Trial and Error

Trial and Error

D. MICHAEL TOMKINS

DODD, MEAD & COMPANY
New York

1 2 3 4 5 6 7 8 9 10

Library of Congress Cataloging in Publication Data

Tomkins, D   Michael.
   Trial and error.

   1. Practice of law—United States. I. Title.
KF300.T63   347.73'.504   80-39757
ISBN 0-396-07944-X

To Prosser, my first law partner, who never asked for a raise—with the knowledge that he will give to Winifred now the same comfort he gave to me.

Chapter 1

Wearing my new three-piece suit, I sat in the hush of a deeply carpeted, darkly paneled reception area. The firm of Skinner, Freeman, and Gates was expanding, I'd heard, and was looking to hire two new associates.

The antique chair was comfortable, and allowed me a clear view of the richly framed portrait of the founder of the firm along with a reflection of myself in smoked glass beside it. I was tired of waiting, tired of listening to the breathy blond receptionist put people on hold. I'd been there since nine forty-five, arriving promptly for my ten o'clock appointment. I'd considered arriving at eight-thirty, but didn't want to appear too anxious. By eleven I was more than a little annoyed.

I was also beginning to have the usual job seeker's feeling that this place was just not me. People had been coming and going for well over an hour, and no one who worked there looked anything like me.

I'd made concessions to the real world since my law school days, but I'd kept my beard. It wasn't that I looked like an anarchist or anything, but on the other hand, I didn't look like I belonged here, either. All the lawyers in this firm seemed to have piercing blue eyes and stand well over six feet. I continued to study my reflection. Short—I was definitely short. "A good size," my mother used to tell me, "a tall five-nine." And in this room, what I had thought was a rich tan appeared only swarthy. My eyes are brown, not blue. The suit helped, of course, but the longer I sat, the less impressive I felt and the angrier I got.

1

I told myself that it was a typical interviewer's ploy, keeping me waiting like that. And I told myself that my feelings were normal ones for the circumstances. But it continued to amaze me that a man who could walk out of his small apartment feeling fit and handsome—well, relatively handsome, anyway—could be reduced to an insecure child, sneaking peeks at himself in a reception room mirror.

At eleven-thirty on the nose, John W. Skinner strode out, grasped my hand firmly, and announced that he would be with me in a quick ten minutes. He disappeared back into his office. Almost true to his word, at eleven fifty-five he again emerged, all six feet of him with paunch, and waved me toward the back. He ran a hand through his abundant silver hair and apologized perfunctorily. Glancing at my resume, which I had sent six weeks before but I'd be willing to bet he hadn't seen until that very moment, he said "So . . . you're looking for a position?"

No, you stupid asshole, I'm a paperweight. "Yes. I've passed the bar and am available to begin—"

"Excuse me," he said, responding to the buzz of his telephone. "Oh, yes, George. Yes, fine. Just a little rain. Yes, I have the file right here." He looked at me, holding up one finger.

I figured it could indicate either a wait of one day, one hour, or one minute. Twenty minutes later he hung up. "Sorry. Where . . . ah, yes. Fine resume, Mac—"

"Mike, Mr. Skinner. It's Mike."

"Yes, of course. Anyway—" He answered the phone again. "Harold! Sorry I didn't get back to you last week . . ." And he was off. Golf, upcoming trip to Hawaii, the state of the stock market.

That's when I started it. I took out my brand-new memo book and wrote across the first page "Shit List. Number One, John W. Skinner."

I swore on his double chin that when I was a successful attorney and had a case against him, I would show him as much discourtesy as possible, be as uncooperative as possible—and if the opportunity arose (for which I would pray daily), I would break his legs.

I left his office during the third call. I'm sure he didn't even notice.

Along with six hundred other would-be lawyers, I had taken the state bar exam after graduating from law school. Some with good grades already had jobs waiting, but most were like me—hopeful, apprehensive, and terribly unemployed.

The results were mailed to us. A thin envelope meant sign up again, better luck next time, dummy. A thick one contained registration forms to join the State Bar Association. It meant that it was time to look for work.

Every morning I would leave my sunny one-bedroom apartment and drive the short distance to the tall steel and glass buildings that housed the downtown legal community to begin pounding on the heavy wooden doors covered with many names. I would walk briskly into the plush outer offices, give the receptionist my warmest, most sincere smile and ask for the hiring partner. He was not *always* out, but never before had I realized that so many attorneys take lunch at ten-thirty in the morning.

Law firms tend to specialize. At least the larger downtown firms do. They do the lucrative tax, corporate, and commercial work. Some of the lawyers within these firms may do some divorce work or personal injury litigation, but rarely do they accept any criminal defense work. It's much too distasteful, and they sense that their corporate clients would object to rubbing elbows with street people in the waiting room. Even if a corporate vice-president, in a fit of pique, hatchets his wife and baby daughter, the firm will usually refer the case to a criminal specialist.

Like the medical profession, the law is moving toward specialization. It's more economically feasible. The law changes rapidly as it becomes more complicated and sophisticated by the day. With the recent profusion of administrative rulings, constitutional due process considerations (from school spanking issues to busing), complex tax reforms, governmental regulations—there is just too damn much to know and to keep current on.

I wasn't sure what my specialty would be, or even if I would end up having one. In fact, at this point, I wasn't even certain why I'd decided to be a lawyer. Certainly, it made my parents happy; but I'm sure I had once had more of a reason than that.

What you learn in the three years of law school is a smattering of many things, so when you get out you're not really prepared to do any one thing well. I thought I'd take the first job I was offered, learn how to be a real lawyer, and then see if I liked the particular field fate had handed me. This was academic, so far. I had no decisions to make, since I'd had no offers. Not a one.

At the end of each day I would come home, bandage my knuckles (bruised from banging on those heavy oak doors), soak my feet, and watch cartoons, fighting off the depression that threatened to engulf me despite the gold and blue summer days.

There was no question about it. I needed a companion—someone who didn't care if I had no job, someone who didn't mind that I'd barely passed Tax and *still* didn't know what the "sum of digits depreciation" was.

The next day, instead of putting my ego on the line, I put an adorable, cuddly fuzzball of a Saint Bernard puppy in the back of my Volkswagen. He was barely twelve weeks old and already weighed thirty-five pounds.

He had saucer-sized feet, a promise of the greatness to come. His rear end didn't seem to have any sensory connection to the front of him; when his front was heading in one direction, it was no guarantee that his rear would follow. In his excitement, he'd make little puddles wherever he walked. His back legs would walk in it while his face registered a vast surprise. Like a human baby, he was composed of spheres. His head was larger than the rest of him and all was round—eyes, nose, ears. His tail—not yet the grand full plume time would make of it—was a dirty white string.

I was the proud father, grinning like an idiot, admiring my new dependent with peeks in the rearview mirror as we headed home. Since I'd never had a dog before, I stopped at the bookstore and purchased an armload of books—all the knowledge I'd need to be an enlightened parent. When I returned to the car, the furry little jerk was in the process of eating a lawbook I'd left in the back seat.

That book, *Prosser on Torts*, is probably the most famous lawbook ever published, and usually one of the first books ever read by a law student. After yelling at the chewing and still unnamed puppy—which caused him to cower with fear and relieve himself on the seat covers—I decided to name him after the author of his first meal with me: Prosser.

This was fitting, I thought, and just. A tort is a civil wrong as opposed to a criminal wrong (which is called, logically enough, a crime). Therefore, tortious conduct includes negligently running a red light so as to cause an accident, punching a hole in your neighbor's head, or slandering an individual by accusing him of having contracted V.D. without benefit of a toilet seat.

So I figured that if the little guy whimpering in the back seat grew up to be a two-hundred-pound muncher of postmen, a name like Prosser would come in handy—if for nothing else than to serve as a contact with the great author himself in case I got sued and needed counsel.

For the next several days I forewent busting my knuckles on law firm doors and took to properly parenting the puppy Prosser. No longer a yo-yo trick, "walking the dog" now meant our meanderings around the commercial area of town where our apartment was located. Prosser loved it. He would sniff busily and urinate, squatting near every signpost. And since he was little enough to get away with it, as well as fuzzy and clumsy, he always drew comments.

"Oh, he's so cute."

"Thank you," I'd say modestly, rubbing my toe in the dirt. "His name is Prosser."

"Prosser? What kind of a name is that?"

"Well, he's named after a law professor of mine who was an expert in dog-bite cases. I figured if he ever brought somebody's leg home—"

"Oh? You're a lawyer? What kind of law do you do?"

Actually I had never thought about it before. But Christ, I'd do anything—including floors and windows. "Oh," I'd reply airily, "I'm in general practice."

"How nice. What firm are you with?"

"Oh, uh . . . I have my own firm. I'm a senior partner. That's why I can take off during the day like this."

"Well," pat pat, "that's certainly a cute little puppy you have there."

"Yes indeed. I hope to bring him into the firm when he's old enough."

"Do you have a card? Never can tell when I'll need a good attorney."

I'd hand the dog lover about fifteen cards, mumbling, "That's all I can spare," and follow Prosser along the street, hoping to be stopped again.

It got so bad that when people didn't stop me to chat "business," I would get damned angry. I started walking in front of Cadillac and Mercedes showrooms, "window-shopping" in the hope that a few wealthy dog lovers would present themselves to us. But then, I figured, if they could afford a car like that, they wouldn't be apt to hire a dog walker for their attorney.

I did start getting some calls from my dog people though. The phone in the apartment would ring. "Mr. Tomkins' office," I'd say, hoping to sound harried, as if my secretary had stepped out for a moment.

"Is this Mike? This is Mr. Williams. I met you last week while you were walking your puppy."

"Why, yes, I remember. Is there something I can help you with?" I'd try to keep from vocalizing my prayer.

"Well, I hope so. Do you do traffic cases?"

And I was off. Slowly—painfully to be sure—but it was a beginning.

My routine changed after I formed the partnership of Tomkins and Prosser. I would pound doors in the morning and lie through any interviews I was lucky enough to get. ("Oh, yes, Mr. Lewis, I would be very interested in doing garnishments and legal research for the first year or so. No, it doesn't sound boring, sir—not at all.")

By early afternoon I was ready to come home to Prosser, whose joyous welcome never changed, even though all I had to report was no bites so far, not even a nibble—and it was still up to him to feed us. I began to worry, as he grew, that his client-getting ability might perhaps be in inverse proportion to his mass; but I didn't tell him this. So out we'd go, looking for business.

I was getting the *State Bar Journal,* which is a self-serving rag for the benefit of the established members of the bar. There was very little information on job openings, but there was an "Over the Bar" column reporting recent deaths of association members. I began awaiting the *Journal* every month and studying that column with morbid interest.

I would call the firm of the recently deceased. "Hello. My name is Michael Tomkins. I'm a recent law graduate, and I was wondering if your firm has any openings now—or perhaps in the future?"

"Well, I don't know. Our Mr. Perry passed away recently, and there just may be a need—"

"Oh, how terrible. I'm sorry to hear that. Do you think I could make an appointment to see the hiring partner?"

This ploy got me interviews, but no offers. Meanwhile, Prosser was doing quite well. Through his contacts we kept food on the table. Blue Mountain kibbles and hamburger— but food nonetheless.

In front of the supermarket one day, I met a young man who had a legal problem with his landlord. The landlord had turned the heat off in his apartment when he was ten days late in paying his rent. He asked if I could help.

"Sure," I said.

"Well, I can't afford too much. How much will it cost?"

"Fifty bucks for half a day."

"God, that's cheap. How come?"

"Low overhead, and besides, this landlord sounds like a jerk." Actually, what the landlord had done was totally illegal, and once he knew an attorney was involved, he'd probably turn the heat on and waive the rent for a bit. I could do it with a phone call, I hoped.

"If your rates are so reasonable, why don't you tell people?"

"You mean like put a sandwich board on Prosser?"

"Why not?"

"Because I'd like to be a lawyer for more than two months, that's why not. It's illegal to advertise." I scratched Prosser's ear. "It's not fair, really. This little problem you have, for instance—a downtown attorney would charge maybe one hundred bucks—"

"Uh-uh. A hundred and fifty retainer. I already checked. So how are you supposed to get clients?"

"How the hell did I just get your fifty bucks?"

He laughed, patted my partner on the head, and told me to call him when I had any news.

There has never been a valid reason for lawyers or any professional to be forbidden to advertise. There is no real difference between a general practice lawyer and a mom and pop grocery store. If a guy walks into any law office, he probably will get an equally good product. However, the difference in fees may be considerable, depending on the lawyer's economic philosophy, overhead, and what kind of car he wants to drive.

I felt that with the country's growing awareness and sensitivity to consumer affairs, it would be only a matter of time before some attorney would bring suit over the question. As it turned out, in 1977 the Supreme Court came down with a ruling allowing attorneys to advertise—but in 1972, no way. Just me and my partner's good looks.

My work load grew slowly and painfully—but it grew. I was attracting fender-benders, wills from the older people I met walking, and other such high-powered cases.

I had placed my name on a list with the Lawyer Referral Panel for the country. This is a clearinghouse sponsored by the bar association as a way of helping the public accomplish the difficult task of selecting an attorney. Instead of searching the Yellow Pages, the client pays ten dollars to the referral office and is given the name of an attorney on the panel.

This is a very select list. The attorneys must fulfill several stringent requirements: They must be able to speak English, must be breathing, and, most importantly, must have the twenty-five dollar sign-up fee.

Although they weren't about to give me the million-dollar personal-injury suit involving the young doctor crushed by the runaway beer truck driven by a drunken teamster, if I could get five or six referrals in a year, I figured it was worth my twenty-five bucks.

The referral office was on the second floor of an old building near the courthouse. While I was filling out the forms I heard pounding.

The receptionist smiled apologetically. "There's a tiny office next door. It has plumbing problems, air-conditioning problems. This always goes on."

"An office?"

"Well, barely. It has exposed pipes—oh it's a mess, all right. We use it for a storage closet."

"Oh." I continued filling out the form. "Do people have to come in here before you get in touch with an attorney, or do they just phone for an appointment?"

"Oh, no. They come in here and we interview them. We have to determine the particular legal problem as well as take the registration fee."

"Must get a lot of foot traffic."

"We sure do. Just look at this carpet. Every year we have to replace it."

On my way down to the building's rental office I thought of how I would break the news to Prosser. He thoroughly enjoyed the client conferences in my plush offices that closely resembled my apartment.

"Mr. Tomkins, is it?" The building manager sat in a small, airless cubicle in the basement, crowded with cardboard boxes. He wore a stained undershirt that strained to cover his vast stomach and didn't quite meet his green work pants. I stared in fascination at the jiggling expanse of white belly covered with thick black hair. His head was totally bald. On his desk sat stacks of old phone messages. Half-eaten jelly doughnuts oozed onto the scratched wood. "Why the hell do you want that hole? We have other vacancies. On Four we have a—"

"I want that one. Is it for rent?"

"I'm not sure." He belched. "It's so small, and it has access to some important ducts. Working on it now, as a matter of fact." He massaged his ample stomach. "You don't really want that one. The one on Four is a—"

"I'll pay seventy-five dollars a month. You don't have to do anything—just paint it, that's all."

"Seventy-five? We were getting ninety from the last guy. He was a salesman for men's furnishings. Transferred to Altoona, or someplace like that. He liked it fine, and paid ninety."

"Eighty dollars," I said, reaching for my checkbook. "That's nine hundred sixty a year. Okay?"

He nodded. "Got yourself a sweet little place there."

I had an office. I had an office next door to the referral office that had to replace the carpet every year. Maybe now Prosser could retire—and maybe, just maybe, in fifty years I could, too.

Chapter 2

The little office was working out well. I had gone to my local bank, to which I had entrusted my $220.15 checking account. Knowing that I had no assets except Prosser (and he was lousy collateral), I was prepared to impress them with the fact that I was now a downtown attorney.

When the loan officer finished yawning I realized that what you are is irrelevant. What you had was all that counted. A simple truth of the new "professional": Balance sheets, not bullshit, got you money.

With the two thousand dollars I managed to borrow with my car as security, I decorated my office in tasteful poor and ordered letterheads printed at InstaPrint, foregoing a rubber stamp on typing paper. I could never get it straight on the page anyhow.

I gave Ma Bell more money than I could afford. "Are you going to want an intercom, Mr. Tomkins?" inquired the bright-voiced customer representative.

Not hardly. "No thank you. It's a small suite."

An established firm, Kaplan, Stein, and Horowitz, was located on the next floor. I vaguely remembered interviewing with them before, but then I vaguely remembered interviewing everywhere in town. I arranged to use their Xerox machine and law library.

My routine changed drastically. Instead of walking Prosser on the city streets, I found myself hanging out alone by the elevators.

"Where is the referral office, young man?"

"Just down the hall on your left—second door. Don't go into the first door. That's my law office."

"Oh, you're a lawyer?"

And sometimes they even went into the first door on their left.

One afternoon while I was waiting for someone to get off the elevator and stumble into my office, Nancy Johnson from the office next door popped her head in. "You busy?"

"Well, sort of. The chief justice of the Supreme Court wants this brief by five o'clock and I'm going to trial tomorrow on a murder case. But go ahead, Nancy, I can spare a couple of days."

Nancy was forty years old, the mother of three, and a new administrator for the referral office. I think she felt sorry for me—the struggling young barrister who worked next door.

She smiled. "I just stopped by to see if you wanted a new case. An elderly lady called in this morning—about a traffic ticket, I think. She wasn't very clear about the problem, but she needs to see someone right away."

I turned over the empty pages of my calendar. "I think I can squeeze her in."

"Thanks, Mike. It's nice of you to take the small ones." Nancy—always sensitive to one's feelings. A real mother in the nicest sense.

The phone rang later that afternoon. "This is Mr. Tomkins. Can I help you?"

"Yes. My name is Edna Carlyle." The voice was quavery, very old.

"Hi, Mrs. Carlyle. Do you need to talk to an attorney about something?"

"No. I need to talk to a lawyer."

"Oh. Well, go right ahead. I'm a lawyer."

"I don't understand about the car. Some men came to my door yesterday, said I did something wrong with my car."

"Do you mean you got a ticket?"

"No. Not a ticket . . ."

"Did you get served with a Summons and Complaint?"

"No, I don't think so. What's that?"

"Listen, Mrs. Carlyle, put down the phone and get the piece of paper that they gave you. I want you to read it to me."

Without further words, she dropped the phone. For several minutes I heard no more sounds.

"Shit," I said to myself, thinking I'd been cut off. Just then I heard a little tiny hello from the receiver I still held. "Mrs. Carlyle? Edna? I thought we'd been cut off."

"Who is this?" The voice was fiery with indignation.

"Mike Tomkins. You called me. I'm an attorney."

"I didn't call you, young man. I picked up the phone and you answered."

"Mrs. Carlyle, how old are you?"

"How old . . . that is absolutely none of your business. You can't just call people up and ask them their age. That's rude."

"Sorry. Listen, Mrs. Carlyle. Let me come over tonight and look at this piece of paper you have. Maybe I can help you figure this out. I can't help if I don't know what the problem is."

"Yes, you come over. I don't know anything about this. I think my neighbors did this. They've always been jealous of my garden."

At six o'clock I drove up to a well-kept little brick house and knocked on the door. I was greeted by a lovely little lady—short and trim with snowy hair and snapping brown eyes behind her steel-rimmed spectacles. Sort of everyone's grandmother. Norman Rockwell would have loved her.

"Mrs. Carlyle?"

"Yes. You must be Mr. Tomkins. Please call me Edna. And come in, come in." She ushered me into a tidy dining room. "May I get you something—a little refreshment?"

Marveling at her self-possession, I settled comfortably into the chair she indicated. "No, thank you."

"Well, if you don't mind, I'll have something." She scurried into the kitchen. "You know," she said, reappearing with a coffee cup and saucer in hand, "I certainly appreciate your stopping by like this." She set the cup on a magnificent mahogany sideboard, from which she withdrew a fifth of Wild Turkey. She laced her coffee generously. "Sure you won't have a little pick-me-up?"

Thinking I'd be sociable, if not professional, I said, "Well, maybe a small something."

Edna reached for a glass and poured me—not one or two fingers but a whole fistful. I resisted the impulse to look behind me to see who else was going to help me drink all that.

"Okay, Edna," I said, "did you find the piece of paper you were looking for this afternoon?"

She nodded, handing me the State Uniform Traffic Citation. It stated that Edna Carlyle had been cited for failure to yield the right of way and hit-and-run. Christ.

"Edna, did you hit somebody?"

She straightened in her chair. "No, never. I never struck anyone in my—"

"I mean with your car. Did you get in an accident on September eleventh?"

"No."

"Did you drive that day at all?"

"Just a little."

"Okay. Did anything happen at around five o'clock?"

"Definitely not." She sounded less indignant, though. "Well . . . except for that car in front of me. But I had the right of way, so I kept on going home. I've been driving for sixty-five years, and believe you me, I know the laws, and—"

"Do you think your car may have made contact with the other car at any time?"

"No. I'm sure of it, except when the wheels touched, but

my car is fine. They didn't hurt it too much except for the scratch on the side." She lifted the bottle. "A little more refreshment, Mr. Tomson?"

"No, thank you. The name is Tomkins. Mike Tomkins. Now, who gave you the ticket?"

"A man came to the door Tuesday."

"Was he in a uniform?"

"No. He was a nice man, had on a blue suit with gold buttons."

This was not going to be fun. A sweet old lady fading in and out of reality. I obviously could not rely on any of her statements as to facts. I just hoped she hadn't hurt anyone in the accident.

Hit-and-run sounds terrible, and it is, but it's less serious if one hits a bumper on a car rather than the hip of a pedestrian. The punishment is an automatic suspension of the driving license for one year, a fine, and a weekend in jail.

As a practical matter, Edna wasn't going to spend any time in the slammer. Not an eighty-six-year-old lady. So if she had in fact hit the other car (and the chances that she hadn't were about the same as my chances of staying sober if I finished the tumbler of Wild Turkey), my job was going to consist of keeping her license and making sure that she received only a small fine.

But first: my fee. Even for eighty-six-year-old ladies—my fee.

"Edna, lawyers are paid to help people in legal trouble, and there's no question you need a lawyer for this."

"How much is it going to cost, young man? I'm on a fixed income, and I don't know how much the insurance company will charge me to fix my car. Don't try and cheat an old lady, Tom."

"Mike. You have insurance on your car?"

"Of course. I've been with the same company for sixty-one years. They know me very well."

I bet they do, I thought. "Well, Edna, I'll call you tomorrow and let you know what I've found out." I rose unsteadily to my feet. "Let me do the worrying." I wove to the front door, stumbled on the step, and with a jaunty wave left the tidy little house with the little old lady inside.

By the next afternoon I found out that Edna had rear-ended a car while making a left turn, slowed down enough to determine that there was nothing askew with her car, and continued home. The driver of the other car had gotten her license number and called the police. The police had delivered the ticket. Thank God no injuries had occurred—and only slight damage to the other car.

"Mrs. Carlyle? This is Mike Tomkins calling like I promised."

"Who is this?"

"Mike Tomkins. I saw you yesterday. I'm an attorney."

"I already have an attorney," she said querulously.

"I know. I'm him. I'm the attorney." I shook my head, feeling as if I'd fallen down the rabbit hole. "I came over to your house yesterday. Remember?"

"Of course I remember."

"Good. Now, Mrs. Carlyle—"

"Goodbye."

"What . . ." The line was dead. She'd hung up on me. Cute was cute, but this was a bit much. I dialed again, annoyed.

"Hello?"

"Edna, don't hang up on me." I spoke fast. "I have to tell you something. This is your lawyer, Mike Tomkins. Just listen to me."

"Okay, I'll listen."

"Good. Now I found out that—"

"*Good*bye." Click.

I'll send her a letter, I thought brilliantly. She can't hang up on a letter. Information will be transmitted and she could refer to it when her mind became a bit cloudy.

I drafted the letter, mailed it that same afternoon, and took the rest of the day off. I felt I'd earned it.

The park was in full use that day—the trees orange and gold in places, with the dappled green of summer not yet given up. Children, families, dogs chasing frisbees—all were there. Prosser and I strolled toward the refreshment stand. I'd planned to buy him an ice-cream cone and one for myself.

He had a little better control over his hind legs by now and could navigate in a generally straight line. He had also reached a majority of his adult size and presented a dignified picture as he paced at my side. He gazed benignly at the other dogs leaping and dashing in and out of the lake, but it never seemed to dawn on him that he was also a dog and such activities were appropriate for himself.

"So this is the famous Prosser." The voice came from a young lady propped under a small tree, her right leg enveloped in an enormous cast. Her crutches lay on the grass alongside.

"Janet! What happened to you?" I'd known Janet Becker casually ever since I'd come to Seattle. She worked at the Velvet Noise, a small bar that was much warmer and nicer than the name would suggest. Everything about Janet used to sparkle, from her glossy black hair to her easy smile. She looked tired and sick now. "Your leg . . ."

"Car accident. About a month ago. I'm stuck with this cast for a while longer, I guess."

"So you're not working now? I haven't been to the Velvet Noise in a while. My practice seems to be taking off, and I don't have the time I used to."

"That sounds like good news," she said with a poor imitation of her usual smile. "You used to hang out there entirely too much, if you ask me. Without me, the place is nothing, anyway. I can't work until the cast comes off, and maybe not then for a while."

"Tell me what happened," I said, sitting down beside her.

"Oh, God, I'm sick of talking about it. Some guy pulled out in front of me. I really like your dog." She scratched Prosser's big head between his ears, getting in return his patented look of adoration. "So now I lost my job. They had to rebreak the leg, and I've got medical bills you wouldn't believe. Not your basic great couple of months."

"Broke, huh? Maybe I can help. Was there any insurance involved?"

She shook her head. "I don't think so. Let me tell you what happened."

After I heard her story of a relatively common car crunch, I said, "Okay, if you don't understand what I'm going to tell you, just stop me and I'll explain it better, okay?"

She nodded her head mournfully, still kneading Prosser's neck.

"In this state you're not required to carry insurance for your car. Certain states do require people to carry it, and you have to prove you do before they'll issue you a license to drive. It has to be in a certain amount. In Idaho, for instance, the amount you have to carry is at least ten thousand dollars. But in Washington, you don't have to carry insurance at all. With me so far?"

"Yes, but I don't know what this has to do with—"

"Wait. The problem arises when you get in an accident that's your own fault *and* you can't pay for the damage. Then the law says you have to have insurance before you can drive again. If you don't get insurance or can't get it, you cannot drive—or anyway, you can't get a license. In other words, it's not real smart to drive without insurance."

"I already know that," she said peevishly, wiggling the hurt leg. "This damn cast itches more than you could believe."

"In your case, Janet," I continued, "it sounds as if the accident wasn't your fault."

"It certainly *wasn't*," she said. "He turned left right in front of me."

"Maybe they can say you should have reacted faster. But basically, no fault of yours. No reason, then, to be reluctant to press your claim."

"Claim? What claim? The kid didn't have insurance. It wasn't his car."

"Does the owner of the car have insurance?"

"I don't know. But the kid said that his friend wouldn't cover him if anything came of it. So I figured I was out of luck." She sat up straighter, her itching leg forgotten. "Mike, are you trying to figure out if there's another way—"

"If the driver's friend who is apparently the owner of the car has insurance, we have a shot at getting you some money. Insurance covers the car itself, not the driver. So if the owner had insurance on the car and he gave the kid permission to use it—what we call a 'permissive driver'—then you can sue him for your damages. Now, if you had insurance, and the other driver didn't, then you could get money from your insurance company under a provision of the policy called uninsured motorist coverage. That means that basically you're buying protection for yourself against other people. That kind of coverage is cheap. And it's very worthwhile. Did you know that thirty-seven or forty percent of the drivers out there are driving around without insurance?"

"I'm duly chastened." A smile flashed, more like her usual impish grin. "Talk on."

"So, now let's see if we can scare up some insurance money for you."

"And if we can't?"

"You're no worse off, right? I'm good at this—not great, but good. If worse comes to worst, we can always sue the driver and hope he's making a quarter-million a year as a heart surgeon."

"Not a chance. He's a nineteen-year-old kid. Works at Pizza Haven as a dishwasher."

"Doesn't sound good. But come into my office. Do you know where it is? Okay, bring all your medical bills and any information you have about the accident and we'll see what we can do."

Personal injury cases can be the most lucrative for a lawyer.

Traditionally a contingent fee is charged. The attorney takes a percentage of any recovery which is made. If there is no recovery made, the attorney charges nothing beyond the costs of trying. That is the upside for the client.

The upside for the lawyer with an arrangement like this is the fact that, in the event of any recovery, he is able to collect a substantial fee amounting to more money than an hourly rate would net him.

Rarely does a personal injury case go to trial. In the event that it does, a jury trial is the method of choice. "Ladies and gentlemen, this poor woman will have to crawl on her belly like a reptile as a result of this accident. Give her money." Juries seldom refuse.

So if there was insurance somewhere involved in Janet's accident, I was likely to be able to get at least some of it.

Janet showed up at my office on Monday, clutching a sheaf of medical bills and a copy of the police report on her accident. Feeling professional, I went to work. A few phone calls to the parties involved gained me the information that the owner of the car did indeed have insurance.

I put in a call to the adjustor. An insurance adjustor is a very important person to the economic life of an attorney, hired as he is to evaluate the case, negotiate with the injured party or the attorney, and recommend a settlement figure. Or maybe even deny the claim outright.

There are several techniques to get a settlement: Sometimes belittling the adjustor works. "Listen, little gal, I've been practicing law for ten years, and I think your analysis of this case is ridiculous and shows that you have very little experience and/or education. Let me speak to your supervisor."

Other lawyers try to compliment, cajole—or beg. "Listen, I've got to make my house payment and the baby needs shoes. Please give me five hundred dollars."

Neither way has ever been effective for me. I've learned

that the best way to convince somebody to do something for you is to identify with them and their problems—and compliment them a little to boot. "I'd like to figure the best way to make your job easier. I know you're good at what you do and have so many of these things crowding your desk. Tell me what I can do to help you."

Adjustors are usually overworked; a good one will be able to close most of the files assigned to him. But all the files are reviewed by a supervisor—a sort of armchair quarterback. The adjustor has to walk the fine line between settling too many files for too much money (by the insurance company's standard), or fail to close too many and have them be referred to the company's defense lawyer.

It's a shitty job, really. Adjustors take an awful lot of crap from an awful lot of people on both sides of a case. I've found that when I treat them like human beings and offer to cooperate with them in any way that I can to make their job easier, they respond like the normal people they are and actually help me do my job better and faster.

There are several types of injury that are compensable. One of the most important is lost wages, which sounds like an easy type to document. But it's not always that easy. How do you document overtime, sick pay, gross income versus net income, a new business without a history of economic productivity, or a new job relying on commission?

I didn't think there'd be any problem with Janet's case, since I was pretty sure she made little more than the minimum wage. Of course, I knew we could kick it up some by adding the value of the free meals she got to eat while working.

I took out my form labeled "Personal Injury Intake," which I'd Xeroxed from the one I'd seen at the firm upstairs. "Okay, Janet, how much do you make?"

"I don't make anything now, I'm not working. But when I worked, I made about fifteen hundred a month."

I stared at her. She sat in my battered secondhand client

chair, twisting a lock of dark hair around her finger. She wasn't smiling. "Listen, Janet. I'm glad you're catching on to the principle of this thing so fast, but I'm the one who'll figure how much to pad it. You just tell me the real amount."

"That's it. Fifteen a month. Sometimes more, but I'd say that's a good average. I make sixty to seventy dollars a day in tips."

"Sixty to seventy a day? And what do they pay you for a salary?"

"God, I don't know. Minimum wage, I expect. I never paid much attention. The money I made was from the tips. I just used my paycheck for food and stuff."

"We'll have to check," I said, making a note to myself to call the manager at the Velvet Noise. "Is it okay if I get a statement from your boss about the wages and hours?"

"Sure. The only thing that worries me is the tax part of it. I mean, we all figured out what to tell the tax people. They make you fill out a little slip every two weeks stating how much you made in tips, you know. And so we all agreed on a figure—like eight or ten dollars a day—and used some number close to that. If one person told the truth, the IRS would sure as hell come in and investigate the rest of us, right?"

"So you never paid taxes on that money you earned, is that what you're telling me?"

She nodded.

"Well, I'm not going to worry about that right now. My main problem is going to be convincing the adjustor that you really made what you say you did."

She shrugged. "I don't have any income tax return to show it, anyhow. I haven't worked there long enough."

"I just can't believe you could make that much money hopping tables."

"Nobody believes it. I've tried to get a loan, like to buy a car. No good. In the first place, waitresses—especially cocktail waitresses—are considered irresponsible. We job hop a lot. That's because the best-money place might change from six months to six months. If you're really good at it, and your legs haven't gone yet, you can jump around and make really good bucks for a few years."

"That sounds like the way old football players talk—'if your legs haven't gone yet.'"

"Yeah, it's like that, I guess. For a while, you can make really good money at it. The problem is that you get fried really easy. People treat you funny. I always pretend I'm somebody else when I'm working. You know, I laugh and giggle a lot. I act like what they want me to be. Then, if this accident hadn't interfered, I was going to take the money I'd saved and go back to school—find something else to do."

"Like what?"

"Oh, I don't know. Maybe early childhood education or something. I'd rather work with little kids than a bunch of drunks."

"Maybe we can get you some money so you don't have to do that any more than you planned."

"Wait a minute, Mike. I don't have the money to pay you to—"

"Don't worry, Janet. The fee out of your pocket is zero. If we get lucky and get you some dollars, then I'll take one-third of what we get. If we get nothing, then you owe me a kiss and a drink, okay?"

"Sounds great to me," Janet said, gathering her crutches and hobbling off. "I'll just send you over all the rest of my bills and things and let you do whatever it is that you're going to do. Call me if there's anything to report."

I worked on documenting Janet's file for the rest of the afternoon. Her medical bills would be relatively easy—I could send the bills to the adjustor. But those alone would not be explanatory of the type of injury and degree of suffering she had incurred. For that, I was going to need medical reports from Janet's treating physician. Those reports, detailing prognosis, diagnosis, an evaluation as to whether the injury is permanent or partial, are the most important documents in a personal injury case.

Short of a trial, that is all the information I could give the adjustor to develop my theory of compensation due. The problem for me was this: It seems doctors hate to write and hate to dictate. More than that, doctors hate lawyers with an unbridled fury, a blinding passion, which in my opinion comes from the fear that a "smart-tongued lawyer" could embarrass one of them in the unlikely event he had to testify in one of these cases.

Clearly, writing an evaluation is a more palatable choice for a doctor than having to testify. The fact is, medicine is not an exact science; the doctor cannot say with any certainty whether or not the patient will fully recover, or when. The best guess is just that, a guess. Pretty heady stuff for the insurance company's defense lawyer.

Doctors avoid the specter of litigation by doing all they can to encourage the lawyer not to count on them for help, even if that help will assure the payment of their bill. One way of not cooperating is by writing a report which plays down the injury, in the hope that the lawyer will become discouraged and go away, accepting a lower settlement figure.

If all else fails, the doctor charges the lawyer an astronomical fee for testimony—two or three hundred dollars an hour to testify, not including waiting or preparation time.

My hope and dream in law school was to room with a medical student, a roomie with whom I could share the trials and tribulations of professional school, someone who would realize that in a few short years we could retire with Mercedes cars and fast women. It was not to be.

Instead I roomed with a tall rosy-cheeked law student from Saginaw, Michigan. His whole family was comprised of doctors, and he didn't like his family; hence he disliked doctors.

At the time I met Janet in the park, I was still following my dream of finding a friendly doctor who would understand that helping me *is* helping his patients; and that I could help him make his patients better, both physically and emotionally by getting good settlements on personal injury cases. Doctors spend so much time filling out forms—insurance forms, state medicare benefit forms, Blue-Cross forms—all types. Why not extend this paper pushing and continue to benefit the patient?

But I had not yet succeeded in meeting the M.D. of my dreams. I had to work with what I, or Janet, had available. I typed out a letter to her physician, requesting that his evaluation of her condition be sent to me in the form of a report, enclosed a copy of the release-of-medical-information form Janet had signed, and tucked her file in the drawer to await the return of the evaluation.

Chapter 3

Edna Carlyle called four days later. Furious. "Mr. Michaels?"

"Tomkins. Mike Tomkins. How are you, Edna?"

"I received your letter the other day. Read it, but I certainly don't understand why you're saying those things about me. You're *my* lawyer, not those other people's. When do we go to court? They say I hit them while I was turning, and I don't want you to delay this any more just to waste time. My car needs to be repaired."

"The court date is at the end of October, Mrs. Carlyle— three weeks from now. But I'm going to need some money before that. Are you going to be able to afford it?"

"Fine, fine. How much?"

"Two hundred dollars," I said, not knowing how this figure would affect her, and beginning not to care.

"Can I give you a check when my Social Security comes?" She sounded calmer now.

"Sure," I said. Wampum, pearls—anything. "A check will be fine. When can I come over?"

"How about tonight, when you finish work?"

"Yes indeed. But please, Mrs. Carlyle—no more Wild Turkey this time. I'm not up to it."

I arrived at six-thirty, apprehensive that the lucid moments would have passed and I would spend an hour introducing myself. "Hi, Edna," I said brightly, as the oak door swung open.

"Yes?"

"Oh, Jesus Christ—Edna, please, you know me, Mike Tomkins. I'm your—"

"Attorney," she chirped. "Please come in. You're so nervous—a shame to be so high-strung at your age."

We retired to the dining room. "Are you a good lawyer?" Edna asked, as she rummaged through a black suitcase she referred to as her purse. "You're not going to take my money and skedaddle, are you?"

"No, no. And I'll do my best for you."

"I can't seem to find my checkbook. I just had it a bit ago. Come along, I think it's in the bedroom."

I followed her into the neatly kept bedroom where she began pawing through drawers filled with pencils, bus tickets, and Hershey bars that couldn't have been less than thirty years old.

My gaze fell on her bureau, on top of which were neatly stacked twenty- and fifty-dollar bills. Lots of them—maybe fifteen hundred dollars in all.

"Edna," I said, pointing, "what the heck is that?"

"Don't be silly. It's money. I use it for groceries."

"You should put it in the bank, not keep it in the house. It's not safe."

"No, I don't have a safe. I keep forgetting the combination. You know, Mr. Michaels, I don't know where I put the checkbook. Just take some of the grocery money."

Now, I'm as honest as the next guy. I detest situations which place me in direct conflict with my honesty. I could scoop up a handful of cash, I thought. She wouldn't remember how much I'd taken—or even that I'd taken it at all. But then, I could go into the children's orthopedic hospital and steal the wheelchair from a six-year-old girl, too.

"No, Edna. I need a check so you have a record of paying me. You know how we all forget things."

"Well, I don't know where it . . . oh, now I remember," she crowed triumphantly, removing it from the closet, where it had been tucked into the pocket of a tweed coat.

I filled out the check, had Edna sign it, and carefully noted on the stub, who, when, and how much.

Edna called me the next morning saying that her attorney was at the door and wanted to look at her car.

"Listen, Mrs. Carlyle. I'm your attorney. What's the gentleman's name? Oh, never mind. Just put him on the phone."

It was the insurance adjustor examining the damage to her car, a 1964 Ford Fairlane, complete with plastic seat covers and less than twenty-five thousand miles on the odometer.

I filled the adjustor in as far as the ticket and the trial date were concerned. He informed me he had already settled the other car's damage for $375.

Several hours later he called me at the office. He was calling from the hospital emergency room. He had twisted his ankle while throwing himself out of the way of Edna's car as she barreled down the driveway to show him the damage.

Apparently, when Edna is backing her car up she can't see over the seat, so she deals with it by not turning around at all, and just going backward.

"It's not serious, Mike, just a twisted ankle. I won't be limping for long. But Mrs. Carlyle won't be driving for long, either."

"Now, let's not be hasty," I said. "There's a good possibility that the court won't take her license away. Her driving record is good and besides, she needs to drive. Without her license, she'd be housebound."

"Mike, Edna's adorable, but she can't drive. I mean, she physically can't do it."

"You're not going to pull her insurance, are you?"

"Well . . ." There was a slight pause. "I'm an adjustor, not an underwriter. Besides, my grandmother is . . . well, listen Mike, do what you can for her. Just tell her not to drive too far or too often. Because if she does . . . well, I've only got two ankles."

"Thanks. We've all got an Edna Carlyle somewhere in our families, I guess."

"One more thing—she thinks I'm her attorney."

"Don't worry—she thinks I'm the adjustor half the time."

"And the other half?"

"She doesn't know me at all."

We both laughed. Nice guy. I hoped his tennis game wouldn't suffer.

I picked Edna up the day of the court hearing. She was dressed appropriately indeed—a printed silk dress, little white gloves, and sensible shoes. She was full of confidence in the system—it would work and "they" would apologize for making her go through all this.

While driving to court from her house, I was apprehensive as to her mental state on this rather important day. Edna, however, sat erect beside me, clutching her black satchel, humming a little tune.

"How long will the trial last, Tom?" she asked brightly.

"Not too long. We may have to wait for other cases to be called."

"Any murderers?"

"Nope. Not today."

"Too bad."

"Yes, I guess it is."

"You'll take care of me, won't you?"

"Sure will."

"You've been nice." She patted my arm. "Do you have any children?"

"No."

"That's nice. What are their names?"

Oh my God, I thought, if the guy in the black robe hears Edna utter one word, she'll never drive again.

As it always is downtown, parking was difficult. Near the courthouse it was damn near impossible. Edna could not walk far, so I pulled up into the no-parking area in front.

"Edna, now listen closely to me, okay?"

She nodded.

"Good. Now, I'm going to let you out right here. I'll go find a parking spot in the next block. I'll be right back. Don't walk down the street or into the building. Just wait right here."

She nodded and waved as I sped off in search of parking. I knew I had just minutes before I would lose her to the crowds and her ageless curiosity. I was back, panting, at the sign in two minutes. No Edna.

Out of the corner of my eye I spotted a gray head bobbing down the street in the ebb and flow of pedestrian traffic. I caught up with her. She was gazing at the tall buildings, a dazed expression on her face.

I took her arm gently. "Okay, Edna. Let's go."

She recoiled. "What . . . who are you? I'm waiting for someone, I can't go with you . . ." She peered closely at me. "Oh, Tom, why didn't you say it was you? Goodness, let's go. It's after nine already."

We hurried into a full courtroom. Municipal court is always crowded. It is the city court, as opposed to the county court. The municipal court has jurisdiction to hear misdemeanor cases, from parking tickets to indecent exposure. The maximum punishment is 364 days in jail and a five-hundred-dollar fine.

The definition of a misdemeanor is any crime with a maximum allowable punishment of less than one year in jail. In other words, the punishment defines the crime. A felony, on the other hand, is punishable by more than one year in jail.

The calendar is called in alphabetical order. But first I wanted to find the people who would have to testify against Edna. Unlike most traffic cases, in this one a police officer would not testify, for no officer saw the accident.

My conversation with the other driver and his wife confirmed my hunch that they were nice folks who didn't want to see Edna lose her license. I explained the possible consequences and they were willing to agree to any "deal" I could get the city prosecuting attorney to go along with.

As usual, he was sitting at his table surrounded by police officers, defense attorneys, and people appearing "pro se" (without an attorney). The din was deafening. "Hey, is this the right courtroom?" "I gotta talk to the judge." "When do I get to testify? I gotta get back to work." Everyone is trying to get the poor bastard's attention before court starts.

After sitting Edna firmly on the front bench where I could keep my eye on her, placing my briefcase on her lap to weight her down so she couldn't get away, I sallied forth into the utter confusion surrounding the city prosecutor.

Phil Stenger, a tall, balding guy who couldn't have been more than thirty-five but appeared older with his dusty, thinning hair and his little paunch, eyed me wearily. "Who you got?"

"Big one today, Phil—murder one."

"Cut the crap, Tomkins. I don't got the time, and you don't got the talent." He smirked.

Always clever, Phil, I thought. "I got Carlyle, Edna. Hit and run."

"Cute. What are you going to do?"

"Phil, listen. . ."

He rolled his eyes. "Here it comes."

"Its a fender-bender. She didn't know contact was made—a lot of traffic. No damage. Well, maybe a little. Could happen to anyone."

"Did you talk to the cop yet?"

"No cop. Just the other car is here. They don't want Carlyle to lose her license. She had insurance—all damage has been paid for."

"So what happened? Any drugs? Drinking?"

"Drinking? Jesus, Phil, she's eighty-six. She eats mashed bananas. Who do you know who's eighty-six and hits the sauce?" My mind flashed guiltily on the water glass full of Wild Turkey.

Phil looked bored. "Okay, pitch it, Tomkins."

"Drop the hit and run. We cop to negligent and failure to yield."

"Why?"

"I just told you. Look, Phil . . ." I lowered my voice. "Right behind you, the lady with the gloves. Look at that angelic face. She's scared witless—first time in court. It's even turned her hair white."

"You're full of it this morning."

"I got nothing else."

"Other car agree? You sure? Maybe she's too old to drive."

"Already spoke to them. No problem. And she had a little accident, that's all. She's still safe on the roads."

"Okay. But I'll recommend a two-hundred-dollar fine."

"Ouch. That's a bit steep. She's on a fixed income—"

"Had to pay you, didn't she? Are you taking her Social Security check?" He lifted his eyebrows.

Low blow. "Okay, Phil. You win. We'll take it."

Since we were going to plead guilty we were called first. I guided Edna to the low wooden swinging door. We went before the judge.

"Don't say anything at all, Edna," I whispered to her. "I'll talk. Just say yes when I touch your arm."

She nodded. "All right. But my attorney should be here, shouldn't he?"

"Not yet. He'll come later, okay?"

We left the courtroom and paid the fine at the cashier's desk. I dropped her back at her home. Just before Edna Carlyle closed the heavy door, she said, "Mr. Tomkins, you're most kind. I really do appreciate the job you did."

I almost wept. She knew who I was; she even called me Mr. Tomkins.

I returned to the office, tossed Janet's file and some books into my briefcase, and headed for the park. Although I'd had good success with cases and referrals from my earlier sojourns with Prosser, and was managing to make rent in addition to food for us both each month, I still didn't really have enough work to fill up a forty-hour week.

And Prosser was bigger now. Although he was lethargic by temperament, he still took being left alone all day as an affront. Now he unfolded himself from the back seat, peering over my shoulder and monitoring our progress through the sunny streets. The back of my neck was getting damp, and so was the headrest.

I was learning that the constant moisture was the downside of having a large and jowled dog approaching adolescence. When he was a little puppy, he couldn't reach the headrest and drooled privately in the back seat. Since I never sat there, it didn't affect me at all. Little humans stop drooling when they get all their teeth, it seems. But Prosser went from drooling to slobbering copiously. I had taken to keeping a small towel on the passenger seat beside me in order to wipe my neck, the way athletes do.

We found a parking place right near Green Lake, which is a gorgeous warm-water spot near the heart of the city. Any warm water around the Puget Sound area is noteworthy, but this lake was a beautiful mecca for joggers, roller skaters, picknickers, and cyclists. We went there often; Prosser did not like cold water and the bathtub was totally out of the question.

It was clear that this was going to be a banner day for girl watching. I located Prosser's tree, a small maple, tied him to the trunk, and spread a quilt in the sun, my briefcase on top. This was to be a working afternoon, I told myself sternly.

After enjoying the sights for a while, I pulled out the advance sheets I had borrowed from the law library. Advance sheets are the latest cases that have been decided in the state courts and then published, in excruciating detail. By reading them, lawyers can hope to avoid making asses of themselves in court by citing or relying on a case that was overturned one month earlier.

After reading two of the most boring cases ever reported, I

checked Prosser. He was lying quietly under the tree, nibbling on a dandelion with his front nibble teeth. A real Ferdinand—and still growing.

The reading material was dry, the sun was soothing. The noises of the busy two-lane highway only a few yards away, screened by bushes and shrubs, made a soothing buzz. I stretched out facing the water.

I awoke to the sound of screeching tires. I was on my feet and running. It's instinctive for a hungry lawyer to run toward sounds such as these. A station wagon was stopped in the street, a brown-white heap of fur beside it. I looked back toward the tree—no Prosser.

When I reached him, he was still—unconscious, but breathing. A thin line of slobber ran from his mouth. I touched his side, feeling like I was going to vomit.

"There's a leash law in this city, buster. That goddamn dog ran right out in front of me . . ." The speaker was a thin man in his middle thirties, wearing a plaid shirt, plaid pants, and a bright yellow blazer. "Is it your dog, or what?"

"Can you help me get him to the car?" I was afraid to move him, but thought I could roll him gently onto the quilt.

"Oh, Christ. If he isn't dead yet, he will be. Just get him out of the way. If he'd been on a leash this wouldn't have happened." The man leaned against his car, gesturing for the benefit of the small crowd of bystanders. "There is a leash law, you know."

I stood, grabbed this reptile by his mismatched plaid shirt, and lifted him off the ground, bending him against his car. "Shut the hell up, you stupid shit. Just stop talking." I let him go, realizing again, with a curious slowness in my mental processes, that I had to get help for Prosser.

The station wagon backed up and sped away. Somebody from the crowd helped me carry the shallowly breathing Prosser to my car; somebody else brought my quilt and briefcase. I don't remember the drive to the pet hospital. I didn't want to think too much about Prosser, gasping in the back seat. Instead, I thought about the man in the yellow coat. I should have choked him when I had the chance.

I pulled into the parking lot of a cedar-shaded animal hospital located about a half-mile from the lake. Leaving Prosser in the car, I ran inside. It was cool and dim; a woman in a white coat was writing something at the reception counter.

"This is an emergency," I panted. "My dog was hit by a car." I pointed to the parking lot. "He's a Saint Bernard."

She stood, pushing a button on the intercom. "Larry, you and Sam get out here stat. I'll be in the parking lot." With the last word, she flew past me, coat billowing open. "How long ago?"

I stood out of the way as two aides carried Prosser into the hospital. They took him into a back room. "You wait here," said the woman, blocking the way with her arm as I tried to follow. "I'll let you know how he is in a minute."

"I'd like to be in with him, if it's okay."

"It isn't," she snapped, and let the door fall shut behind her.

It was the longest fifteen minutes. I thought again about Mr. Plaid. Now I was sorry I'd grabbed him. I hate violence, I really do. I'd only had two fights in my life—both of them before I was twelve. I'd lost both. Grabbing somebody that way was definitely not in character for me. I found it hard to believe I'd done it. But I must have. I had his button still clasped in my sweating hand.

I waited. Dogs were yelping somewhere in the back of the building, but I could hear no sound from behind the door where Prosser was. I dropped the button on the waiting-room table, next to an old copy of *Vet World*.

One of the young men came out finally, and sat down beside me. "He's going to be okay," he said, smiling. "The doc'll be out in a second to tell you what's happening, as soon as she finishes setting his leg. It's broken."

Something loosened in my chest, and for a moment, I

wasn't sure my voice would work. "Is there anything else hurt?"

The kid was very young, not more than sixteen. He stood up to leave, scratching his shoulder. "Don't think so, but she says she wants to do some X-rays on his head later. He'll probably have to stay here for a while."

It was only a short time later that the vet herself came out. She took off her coat and laid it on a chair, sat down facing me and didn't say anything for a while. I didn't either.

She was about twenty-six, tall, with long auburn hair, straight and glossy, which hung like a tassel and swung with every moment. Her face was angular, with dark eyebrows straight and sharp across the freckled forehead. She wore jeans and a denim shirt.

"You're very lucky," she said quietly. "He's got a broken femur and possibly a concussion and internal bruising. But as far as I can tell now, not much other actual damage. Of course, he's in shock and that's always dangerous. I'd like to keep him here for a few days to monitor his condition."

I felt like kissing her hand, flinging my cloak across mud puddles for her to walk on. Instead, I babbled. "I can't thank you enough. I don't know what I would have done if—"

"Yes. Well, if you're going to take on the responsibility of a large animal, you have to be prepared to *be* responsible. And in the city, that means a leash." She moved toward the reception desk. "Now, let's get him admitted. The boys are preparing the X-ray machine, and I'd like to get started."

I followed her, feeling as if I were six years old again. "But I had him on a leash. Somehow when I was asleep at Green Lake, he got loose and headed for the highway—"

"Uh-huh. Name?"

"Don't you believe me?" I felt like an idiot. Why did I care whether or not she believed me? Because I felt guilty that Prosser got loose? Sure, but having her believe that I was responsible and did care about him wouldn't make anything better.

"Of course I believe you," she said patiently. "Name?"

"His or mine?"

She sighed. "Look, it's been a busy day for me and I'd like to get this over with as quickly as possible so I can work up the pictures on your dog. I need to know who *he* is so I can use his name to comfort him in there. I need to know who *you* are so I can have someone call and let you know when to pick him up, okay?"

Okay. She was gorgeous and snippy and very, very professional. As long as she'd saved Prosser's life, I guessed nothing else mattered very much. I got him registered without further delay. I wanted to tiptoe back inside to let him know I'd visit every day, but the doctor didn't feel it would be a good idea. "He's sedated now and wouldn't even know you were there," she told me, just before she handed me her card and reached for her white coat.

I decided to try once more. "Judith Latimer, D.V.M.," I read from the small card. "Do people call you Judy?"

"No," she answered, pulling on the white coat and disappearing through the swinging door. "They call me Doctor."

The apartment was awfully large without Prosser. It was lonely, too. His dishes sat empty on the floor, the newspaper under them covered with a layer of dried slobber. His favorite toy, a teddy bear kissed almost to extinction, lay abandoned on the floor by the couch. I picked it up, tucked it gently into the corner by the phone, and stared at the wall.

Prosser was alive—with a broken leg, true—but alive. He would be home in a few days. But how would I make it until then? We'd always watched the evening news together while we ate dinner. I'd tell him about my day. The silence was oppressive.

I tried to work, but Janet's case didn't interest me. I couldn't concentrate. I reached for the phone.

"Mike!" Janet sounded as bouncy as her old self. "Am I glad to hear from you. I've been wanting to stop by with some more bills, but just haven't had a chance to get downtown. Taking the bus with these crutches is unbearable. I postpone errands as much as possible. Dr. Sherman says the cast can come off in a week or ten days . . ." There was silence. "Why are you so quiet?"

I told her about Prosser, finding myself wanting to talk about it. I ended up going to Janet's house and having dinner, telling her stories of Prosser when he was a little puppy, and drinking far too much.

Janet didn't question, just listened and fed me. She kept the glass at my elbow filled, too, and tucked me in on her lumpy couch when I was all talked out.

I left at dawn, awakened by the tentative shafts of buttery sunlight creeping through her white curtains. Janet didn't awaken as I tiptoed to the door.

I devoted almost all the remaining week to settling Janet's case. She'd gently refused when I asked her to dinner the following night. "No, Mike, it wouldn't be a good idea," is all she'd tell me. But I had good feelings about her and still felt that they were reciprocated. She was a gentle lady who knew how to give comfort when I needed it. She'd been a good friend to me when I was hurting, and now I was going to get her the best settlement that could be got.

Sometimes the question is raised as to whether people really need lawyers to help them get an insurance settlement, or whether that's another of the self-serving myths perpetuated by the omnivorous bar association.

The reality as I see it is that when you are negotiating with an adjustor or another attorney you are talking about the relative value of a soft-tissue injury, say, or a broken leg. How does one know what a particular injury is worth?

Attorneys and insurance people know better than most people, but still it can be tricky. You can't look up an injury in a catalog: "Hey, Jack, what's a simple left ankle break, sprained wrist, and stitches in the forehead going for nowadays?"

"Male or female?"

"Male."

"Athlete?"

"No."

"Permanent partial?"

"Four percent, to the leg."

"Okay, I got it. Call it sixty-eight hundred."

"Good. I'll take two. My wife wants one."

It doesn't work that way. I know an adjustor who settled a wrongful death claim of a forty-five-year-old construction worker for $472 burial expenses plus fifteen hundred to his wife to "go buy yourself two weeks in Florida—get away for a while, ma'am." Any lawyer in the world would have done better for this unfortunate lady.

The fact is that when an attorney is involved in a personal injury claim, his mere presence increases the worth of a claim immediately by at least fifteen percent. Maybe that's not how it should be, but that's how it is. Insurance companies don't make a profit by paying more than they feel they have to.

What the client is purchasing with the contingency fee in cases like this is the ability to bullshit. Judgment, ability, and bullshit—and not necessarily in that order—are the qualities allowing the attorney to know what to say to the adversary or what not to say, whom to talk to, and whether to get a doctor's report.

Janet was lucky. She'd picked a doctor who, judging from the report I'd received from him, knew how to write. It even wrung my heart, reading about the pain that kept Janet awake nights, the course of physical therapy she'd have to undergo once the cast was off, the psychological stress that being even temporarily disabled caused her.

The adjustor at Northwest Casualty was an older man, Ellis Gresham. He hadn't been there long, was overworked as all adjustors are, and was positively compulsive about having his file documented. I put in a lot of time talking to him on the phone about which piece of paper I was going to send next.

"Mr. Gresham? Mike Tomkins." I arranged the file in front of me, carefully squaring it to the edge of my desk. The phone was cradled on my shoulder.

"Ah, yes. The file is right here. I received your last demand letter, Mr. Tomkins. I had my supervisor review the file. He felt your demand is way ouf of line, frankly."

"I don't see why," I said smoothly. "I thought that based on the doctor's reports and the possibility of permanent partial disability of the leg, even after therapy, that the demand was low. I made it low so we could settle this damn thing without a trial."

"Oh, I wish we could, too, Mr. Tomkins. I really do." Ellis paused. "But the numbers don't look right."

"It's funny you should use the word *look,* Ellis," I said. "I saw Janet this morning. The cast was removed a few days ago, and her leg looks awful. It's a shame. Have you ever met Janet, Ellis?"

"Uh, no. No, I haven't."

"Very pretty lady. Super legs—well, anyway, one super leg. I'll probably want mostly women on the jury, have her walk into court with a short skirt, limping slightly. No nylons. She'll make a super witness, you know. Articulate, understated. Did I say she's quite attractive?" I waited.

"Okay," Ellis said after a moment. "The point is made. But her wages—future disability which is totally speculative. No way can I give you $32,000."

"What can you give me to avoid trial?"

"Fifteen tops. Maybe not even that."

"Bullshit. That's just crap, Ellis." I shifted the phone to my other ear. "Tell you what. I come down nine, you come up nine. We settle this thing now. That way you get a closure, I get to feed my dog. It's a fair settlement for such pretty legs."

"I can't do it."

"Okay." I waited.

"Five more—twenty thousand. And I'm going out on a limb, Mike. Way out."

"Twenty-three?" I crossed my fingers.

"Nope."

"You're going to go to trial over two thousand dollars?"

"If we have to," said Ellis, unperturbed. "Take it or file suit."

"Great legs," I mused.

"Twenty-two thousand, five hundred. Don't say another word."

"Send me a check, Ellis."

"You're certainly unorthodox, Mr. Tomkins."

"I'm just crazy about good legs," I told him. "Drop by sometime. I'll buy you a warm beer."

Jesus. Just like they never taught you in law school.

Janet came to the office to pick up her check. Except that it was somewhat paler than the other, the hurt leg looked as good as new. "It feels a little shaky sometimes," she told me, "but basically I can get around as well as I ever did."

"It looks terrific," I said, meaning it. "Here's your hard-earned money." I handed her a check along with a detailed breakdown sheet. I'd taken considerable pains typing the damn thing so the columns were neatly centered on the letterhead.

The huge sum of $22,500 stood proudly at the top of the breakdown sheet. While I was typing it, I kept thinking of the *real* worth of my services. I could justify one-third of this figure as an attorney fee to anyone except myself. All doctors' fees were going to be paid—twenty-two hundred dollars of them; so was the hospital and therapy bill. These people all provided a real service. Janet would walk without a limp on two great legs. That kind of result people will gladly pay for.

There was no question in my mind that I did a hell of a job. The settlement was achieved in a timely manner without trial. But still, $7,500 was a nice chunk of money for bullshitting on the phone with Ellis. And the accident hadn't hurt my leg at all.

Janet read over the breakdown sheet, eyes sparkling as she

saw what was going into her pocket. Then she frowned. "Good legs discount?" She pointed to my typing. "I thought your fee would be one-third—seventy five hundred dollars. But here, after the discount, you're only taking six thousand."

"Well, that kind of discount is given all the time . . . if you have good legs," I said.

"And a good attorney?"

"It helps," I said modestly.

She sat back in her chair, twisting a tendril of the shining hair around a finger. "Look, Mike, you're a good person. And I think you're going to be a good lawyer. So, because we're friends, I'm going to be honest with you and tell you a little bit about business. You're starting out, been to college and then to law school and all—but now it's the real world for you. It's been the real world for me since I left high school.

"Business should remain business. We had an agreement. Now you're changing the rules at the last moment. Never mind that it's in my favor," she said briskly as I tried to interrupt. "I'm a proud lady, and I don't like to be in somebody's debt, even if that person is a very nice man. I wouldn't expect to give you more than one-third of the settlement even if we'd had to go to trial and appeal it two or three times. And I wouldn't expect you to ask me to." She looked around the room, taking in the tasteful decor. "I don't see any Picasso originals or rosewood paneling. At this point in our lives, you need this money more than I do. It was a sweet gesture, but not a good one. Okay?"

"So when did you marry a Rockefeller?" I must have come across as a little testy.

"Actually, Mike, next month I'm going to Alaska to work on the pipeline and will be moving in with my boyfriend. I've been in Seattle long enough to figure things out. That's what I want to do. It's hard to figure things out when you're unemployed and hurting, and I thank you for being there for me when I really needed someone to lean on a bit."

"Oh." I stared at her. "I thought—I mean, I know you like Prosser, and I didn't think you were going with anybody . . ."

She smiled, a big, sunny, toothy grin. "God, do I love that dog. Promise if you ever make it up to Soldotna, Alaska, that you'll bring him along." She handed me the breakdown. "Here, redo this, please—without the discount. And then you can take me out to lunch. In all honesty, this office is a downer. Buy me a steak—out of your fee."

"Only if I don't have to retype this damn thing again. You have no idea how much time I put in on getting those columns straight."

Janet was a nice lady. I would miss her.

Chapter 4

I needed a secretary. It was now clear that with things picking up the way they had been, I could no longer be expected to answer the phone when I was in or entrust callers to the tender mercies of the Acme Answering Service when I was out. The last time I'd called in for my messages, the operator had trilled, "Oh, I'm sorry. Mr. Tomkins isn't in."

"This *is* Mr. Tomkins," I told her.

"No, this *isn't* Mr. Tomkins, this is the answering service." I could hear the turning of a page. No doubt she was reading a gothic novel.

Typing was getting to be a problem, too. By the time I'd run some of the longer things out to the suburbs where a married and housebound lady named Mrs. Turner charged me by the page, then had run them back downtown to the Speedi-Print to have copies made, then had trotted back to the office where I stuck the copies in the files and stuck stamps on envelopes, I'd decided that was just not what I'd planned to do with my life, that's all.

The Janet settlement had given me an almost carbonated feeling inside my chest that just might have been the beginnings of confidence. For the first time, I'd made an appreciable sum at lawyering. It was time to act like a real lawyer— and that meant having a secretary.

I knew just what I wanted. I wanted a secretary like the ones in all the movies. You know the movies I mean—the bigwig comes in and she's already there, at her desk. She jumps up, takes his coat, trilling, *"Good* morning, Mr. Bigwig. Here are your messages. I'll have your coffee in a second."

"Ah, yes. Good morning, Mary," says the boss. Whereupon he goes into his office, closes the door, and . . . Well, I don't really remember what he does in there.

Anyway, I knew what I wanted—a secretary just like that. Only pretty. No hair in a bun and orthopedic shoes. And somebody who'd laugh at my jokes. And who didn't chew gum.

I pulled my legal pad closer, uncapped my pen. "Learn legal," I started. Good ad so far. That was a delicate way of saying that I couldn't afford an experienced legal secretary. I figured that if I had to train somebody, I'd be able to teach her things *my* way. I'd just never let her know that everything I knew had been gleaned from old Rock Hudson movies. "Young lawyer desires person Friday." That and the phone number should do it.

The ad drew an incredible response. A cross section of the unemployed came calling. I was beginning to enjoy this. By Friday I'd narrowed it down to Debi (yes, one *b* and an *i*), who was from Texas. She was tall and blond, tanned. ("I ski and play tennis," she'd giggled, "but not at the same time.") She wanted to become a legal secretary so she could "meet interesting people." Then there was Virginia, from the state of the same name. *She* wanted to go into legal work because her fiancé planned to attend law school. That way, she told me, they'd have something to talk about when he graduated. Virginia had dark hair and the most languid, softly husky drawl I'd ever heard. I liked both of them, and by Friday afternoon had determined that I'd have them both come in on Monday to take a typing test.

I notified the answering service (for what I hoped was one of the last times) that I was leaving for the weekend. As I checked the lights and slammed down the one window that opened, I heard the outer office door open softly.

A tall woman, dressed in a tweed suit and soft blue blouse,

was standing in the anteroom. She was about fifty, with wavy gray hair. "Are you Mr. Tomkins?" At my nod she crossed the room, extending her hand. "I'm Jean Campbell. I'm here to see about the job."

In later months, I was to realize the significance of the fact that she did not say, "I'm here to *apply* for the job." Jean always says exactly what she means, no more and no less. But I didn't know that then. All I knew was that she wasn't what I had in mind—not at all.

And I had to get rid of her quickly and go pick up Prosser. The animal clinic closed at five-thirty; I was certain that Judith Latimer, D.V.M., would close the doors, bolt them, and fill the moat right on the stroke of the half hour— especially if she was expecting me.

Still not realizing I wasn't in charge here, I said, "Ah . . . Mrs. Campbell . . . I'm afraid I've pretty well decided on somebody . . ." My voice trailed off as she swept by me and settled herself in the client chair in front of my desk.

She set her purse on the floor beside the chair, removed a steno pad, bounced an experimental couple of times as if testing the springs. "You've just moved in, Mr. Tomkins?"

"Well, not exactly." This was one nosy old broad. I took the chair behind my desk. "I'm not interviewing any more. As I said, I've got someone in mind."

She nodded pleasantly. Her eyes were very blue; they crinkled at the corners when she smiled. "What kind of practice do you have?"

"She *was* pretty old, I thought. Old enough to be my mother, in fact. Maybe she was deaf, a little hard of hearing. I pitched my voice a few decibels louder. "You wouldn't be interested. I represent muggers, robbers, drunks." I hated to be so brutal with a nice older lady, but desperate times require desperate measures.

"Um-hmm." She made a note on her pad. "You recently passed the bar? Good. Now let me ask you this: Where do you want to be in five years? What kind of practice do you want to have by then?" She smiled. "Go ahead, Mr. Tomkins. Let your mind go free for a moment."

I was speechless, but not for the reason she thought. I did not like this woman, not one little bit. "Listen here, Joan—or whatever your name is—"

"Jean," she said pleasantly.

"Whatever. Anyway who's interviewing who?"

"Whom."

"Whom, then. Anyway, you can't just come in here and begin interrogating me at the end of a long day when I've already almost picked out somebody to fill the job. Good God, next you'll be asking *me* for a resume."

"No," she shook her head. "You're far too young for your past to hold any interest for me, Mr. Tomkins. It's your future I'm interested in. I've worked in law offices for a long time, always coming in when the groundwork had been laid, the practice formed. I'm at the point in my life when I'd like to be a party to beginnings."

I could see that this old turkey was going to require a turndown worthy of Kissinger. "Listen, Mrs. Campbell, I'd like to stay and chat with you a little longer, but it wouldn't be fair to you."

She bit. "In what way, Mr. Tomkins?"

"This is a terrible position. It doesn't pay much more than minimum wage. It's really for a kid just starting out. You know, somebody living at home, somebody working for clothes money. There's no sense talking further, you couldn't afford to take the job." With that, I stood up and edged toward the door, hoping she'd follow my example. I'd help her into the elevator, push the down button, even call her a cab if necessary.

But she didn't move. "Your assumption is as unfounded as it is impertinent. Your ad was rather clear as to the amount of experience you were willing to pay for." She twisted in her chair, taking in the chipped walls of institutional green and the linoleum floor, the secondhand steel desk and mismatched filing cabinets. "Or *able* to pay for, as the case may be. The premise of this interview is that I am able to consider taking the offered job at the stated salary and *you* are able to pay it. At this point, the financial arrangements of either of us remain private and—"

"This is *not* an interview. I am interviewing the two people I have chosen on Monday. I'm late for an appointment now." I didn't like this woman at *all*. It was worth not locking the office door to be rid of her.

I fled to the hall. As usual, the aged elevator groaned its way to the sixth floor with more noise than speed.

She joined me. "I must apologize, Mr. Tomkins. I feel I was a little bit rough on you in there."

Through clenched teeth, I repeated, "This is *not* an interview."

"Of *course* it isn't, Mr. Tomkins," she said soothingly. "I think I was so pleased to find a young lawyer such as yourself—someone with a bright future and an uncertain present—I think that so pleased me that I got a bit carried away with the feeling that I might make myself useful. Will you accept my apology, please?"

I nodded, looking at her feet. She didn't wear orthopedic shoes, but black kid pumps with a slender heel. She walked like a woman who'd worn heels daily, with an unwobbling confidence which matched her speech.

The elevator arrived. With a gesture of gallantry born of my certainty that she would be gone from my life in a matter of mere minutes, I pulled the rusted gate and pushed the down button.

"I can certainly understand why you were upset, Mr. Tomkins," she said, staring carefully at the steel doors of the elevator. "It's a very important moment in your career, hiring your first secretary. Handled properly, this decision could result in a shape and direction to your practice that will stand you in good stead until retirement. On the other hand, an unfortunate decision now could mean wasted years all around."

The old bat sure had a gift for drama. And all this time I thought I was looking for somebody to trill good morning to me and bring me my messages. "Uh-huh." It was flowery, but there was something to what she'd said. It might be a good thing to have a secretary who knew things—although I still couldn't figure out why someone with the experience she said she had would want to work for such low pay.

I looked at my watch. "Damn!"

"Missed your appointment?"

"Yeah. And Judith Latimer, D.V.M., will be closing the doors in five minutes. No way I can drive to Magnolia in five minutes. Damn!" I glared at Jean. "I *told* you I wasn't interviewing, now I'll never be able to get Prosser out today—"

"Who is Prosser? Who is Judith Latimer, D.V.M.?"

"Prosser is my dog. He's been in the hospital for a long time, and I was supposed to get him out tonight. Judith Latimer is the vet." The elevator ground on with perverse sloth.

"There's a phone in the lobby, Mr. Tomkins. Couldn't you call and tell her you're on your way and ask her to be patient just for a few minutes?"

"You don't understand. This is a *very* starchy D.V.M."

"I see." She pondered this in silence, but not for very long. "Well, since I am indirectly responsible for your predicament, I will help you to resolve it."

"Indirectly!"

"All right, then. Totally responsible for your predicament, if you insist. Give me the name of the hospital, and I'll call while you get your car and start on over there. What kind of a dog do you have?"

"Prosser is a Saint Bernard. She won't wait for me, I've told you—"

"I think she will. I have a Great Dane, myself."

"You do?" I looked at her with new respect. She didn't look like the type. "What do you do about his exercise?"

"I run him at the beach. It's difficult, isn't it, to find suitable playmates for him—his size, you know. What's the name of the clinic?"

"West Sound Animal Clinic. But she won't wait."

"We can try." Jean gave me a push as the elevator gasped to a halt on the first floor. "Run along now, Mr. Tomkins. I'll take care of Judith Latimer, D.V.M. I'll tell her you're on your way. It's been nice talking to you, Mr. Tomkins."

"Thanks a lot," I called over my shoulder as I ran for my car. Even if Judith Latimer, D.V.M., wouldn't keep the clinic open another fifteen minutes, at least I was making a respectable getaway from the old broad and her desperate longing to be my secretary. Actually, I thought, people who owned large dogs generally were nice types. It would be nice for Prosser to have a friend other than me, a friend who could run with him and wrestle on the sand.

Gravel crunched under my tires as I skidded into the parking lot of the clinic. The lights were still on, and through the large front window I could see Judith Latimer, D.V.M., talking on the phone and running a hand through her auburn hair. It looked to be an absorbing conversation; when I tapped on the front door she looked up in annoyance and pantomimed a moment's wait. Presently she put down the phone.

"That was your secretary," she said, letting me in. "She has a problem with her Dane that sounds a lot like hepatoencephalopathy to me. It's a liver problem. Her regular vet's out of town. I've phoned in a prescription to hold her until he returns on Monday. But she should get him in first thing." She removed a jingling bunch of keys from her leather belt. "I've never seen a case of hepatoencephalopathy since I left school." She sounded wistful when she said that, and also proud that she could say it at all.

"That wasn't exactly my secretary," I said, following her toward the kennel door.

"Well, whoever she is, she said to tell you she'd be a little late on Monday, since she's going to run her dog in to have him looked at." She unlocked the kennel. The smell that never quite left the place hit my nose at the same time barking began from a few score doggy throats.

I could hear Prosser—deep slobbery barks of joy. I felt like barking with joy myself. He ran toward me as soon as she opened his gate, tearing away from the leash. His front paws thudded into my chest, knocking me flat. Then he walked up and down the length of me, ignoring my feeble cries of "Prosser, heel."

"He isn't going to pay any attention to *that*," said Judith Latimer, D.V.M., with scorn. "He's probably not sure where your heel is, with you in that unnatural position."

The position did feel a bit unnatural, at that. My head was wet with Prosser's kisses. I disengaged myself, brushed myself off, and tried to look dignified. That was difficult, with the broad grin of delight refusing to leave my face. "He looks great."

"Yeah, doesn't he? He's a pretty baby," she said, grinning too and tousling Prosser's head. "He was one of my best patients—just waited patiently for you to come and bring him home." She turned toward the reception area. "You should make sure you don't betray that trust again, Mr. Tomkins."

That was the last straw. "Has this been a particularly bad day for you, doctor, or do you make it a habit to make judgments right and left—"

"He was allowed to run in front of a car, that's all I need to know. That will be four hundred nineteen dollars. Cash."

Prosser was busily sniffing the cuffs of my pants and the tops of my shoes. I suspect he wanted to determine where I had gone without him. "Okay, okay. Here's a check. But I am responsible. He was leashed. I care for this dog more than I have to justify to you."

She took the check, put it in a drawer without looking at it. "Sorry. It's been a long day. You can't imagine—old ladies with toothless cats, a parakeet with an eye infection, and then I lost a beagle under the wheels of a pickup truck."

"Professional hazards?"

"We all have them, I suspect."

"And I suspect you need a drink—and something to eat."

"Is that an invitation?" She smiled tiredly.

"Eight years of college, huh? Yes, that is an invitation. I'm excited about getting my puppy back, I made payroll this month, you're tired and hungry—and I think I'm going to like your company."

She gave me an appraising look. She examined me with more care than the situation warranted.

I hate the first time you ask someone out, the little hard fist that appears in your tummy, the little wet spot in your palms. I hoped she wouldn't give me a lame excuse like she had to take a sputum sample from a cocker spaniel.

Once when I was in college I asked a pert little cheerleader to accompany me on what I envisioned as a fun date. She stared at me in the way that Judith was staring now and said, "No thank you, Mike. I don't think we'd have a very good time. I'm complimented you asked, but I don't think so." It was clean and neat, and guaranteed that I'd never ask again. Sometimes ladies really are busy all the time. How the hell do you know?

Judith stood, unbuttoning her white lab coat. "Okay. Bring your puppy and I'll lock up." She was wearing white pants and a navy blue sweater which made her gray eyes look blue.

Prosser bounded out into the parking lot, favoring his right leg ever so slightly. He broke away from the rope leash I had in my hand, jumping on his hind legs like an unbroken mustang. The evening air smelled of evergreens, and the sound of barking could be heard from the kennel.

"I've been told that it stops when we drive away," said Judith, "but it bothers me every night, leaving them like that."

I took her to a quiet little restaurant (does anybody ever take anybody to a noisy big restaurant?) sitting on the water. Prosser was left to snooze in the car. It was sunset, and we had a clear view of the sailboats docking, their running lights coming on. Gulls swooped in for a last wheeling foray before dark.

Judith was a handsome lady, I thought, as we ordered fried zucchini. "Thank you for Prosser," I said, lifting my glass. "I owe you one. Free will, free divorce—you name it."

"Free divorce?" Her mouth curved in amusement. "I doubt I would need that. At least for a long while."

"Ever come close?"

"Once. Maybe . . . I'm not sure. I was a senior in college. I was either going to get married or go to vet school. I still thought I had to choose like that. Either-or."

"Regrets?"

She shrugged. "Not now." She stirred her wine with a forefinger. She looked up, smiling brightly. "What's the difference between a lawyer and an attorney? I've never understood why there are two words for the same profession."

"That's one hell of an icebreaker."

"Well, you know—all the books tell you that in order to be considered charming, you get the other person talking about himself."

"Well, as it happens," I said, "I've researched that very question at considerable length. I've concluded they're one and the same."

"I don't think so. If they were the same, there wouldn't be two words."

"I'm the liberal arts major. You're into science and chemistry and things like that. I can't take your word for it."

I found Judith surprisingly easy to talk to, and surprisingly animated. She had a good appetite, too—a quality I appreciate in people. In the usual fashion of people alone together for the first time, we exchanged our respective life histories.

Judith was the first daughter of a prominent Iowa biologist. She had three younger sisters, all of whom married right out of high school and began producing babies at an astonishing rate. Her father was a hero to Judith during her young life—and a hard act to follow, I gathered. Her childhood was happy and the family was still close.

"Then why are you in Seattle?"

"It wasn't my first choice," she said. "I wanted to work in the Yerkes Primate Center, but my application was turned down. Do you know anything about the work that's done there?"

I nodded. "Some. Isn't that the place where they do the experiments with the monkeys? Teaching them to talk or play chess or something?"

"Uh-huh. But more than that. There are some fascinating things they're doing with learning patterns—things that can help us understand a lot about the development of learning in humans."

"So you came here . . ."

"Yes. I needed to be on my own, to earn a living without the help of my family."

"But can't you apply to Yerkes again?"

"I have." She crossed her fingers, smiling. "I'll be notified in the spring. It's more competitive than anything I've come up against so far."

"Don't you like what you do now?"

"No. No, no, no. Pets. I don't know why I should devote my time as a scientist to the care of overweight animals, most of whom eat better than the majority of the people in the world, when there is so much I feel I could contribute through science. Does that make sense?" She leaned forward, touching my arm. "Can you understand that?"

"I think I can," I said, watching the waiter approaching the table hesitantly. The poor guy was confused, I suppose, as to whom to present the check to. Nowadays, it must be quite easy to offend one or the other of the parties. I waited to see if he was a candidate for a U.N. opening or the boor of the year. He placed the buff check, face down, in the middle of the table.

"I had a surprisingly good time," said Judith, as we drove toward the clinic.

"Surprisingly?"

"Yes. I had mixed emotions. But then I figured that some-body who owns a dog like Prosser couldn't be all bad—even if you don't care for him properly."

"I'm glad we did this," I said. "And now that I have a few paying clients—including one who can't remember my name or much of anything else half the time—maybe we can do it again." I told her about Edna, making it light and, I thought, amusing. I told it with flourish and gusto, waiting for her laughter.

It didn't come. She sat straighter in the seat. "Do you mean to tell me," her voice was tight, "that you represented a lady, knowing that she hit a car, knowing she shouldn't be allowed to drive—and you think it's a funny story?" She shook her head. "God, some people hate lawyers reflexively—and now I'm beginning to understand why." She peered out of the window, no doubt judging the distance back to the clinic.

"Wait a minute, Judith. Am I supposed to take only people who are virtuous, meritorious, and innocent?"

"What did you charge her?"

"Less than anyone else would have."

She said nothing, only reaching back to pat the still snooz-ing Prosser.

The silence unnerved me. "Look, Judith. I don't want to get into a discussion of situational ethics here, but I'm not going to turn down any case for probably four years. Every one that's offered to me, I'm going to take. I can learn some-thing from all of them—and making judgments isn't a luxury I can afford right now. I'm not even sure I'd feel right making the judgments if I could afford to. But right now, it's more a question of economics. I don't make those value judgments. I don't ask my landlord or my phone company to get paid based on some sense this particular case shouldn't be worked . . ." I was beginning to sputter. I stopped, wondering how the evening, which had been going so well, could have deteriorated so fast.

"It seems to me that you have some responsibility toward the public, if only to see that they are protected from some glib, fast-talking attorney."

"What does that mean?" I was getting more and more annoyed. "Maybe your business doesn't present as many situations to be judgmental about as mine—but think about this: What if an owner comes into your clinic with a dog who had been hit by a car. You know that this particular dog has bitten several children, a nun, and two social workers. Would you—"

"That's the dumbest analogy ever—"

"Just answer the question."

"I can't. It's apples and oranges. I heal sick animals."

"And I put diseased people back in society."

"It's a combination. Not only do you take cases and get people off without thinking of the victims, but you help people get money they don't deserve. Oh, I don't know."

"Listen, Judith. Money made you a doctor."

"Yes, but I think your profession fattens on the misery of other people."

"Just for the sake of argument, what's wrong with that?" I really wanted to know, since this was an argument I'd had with myself several times already. I could argue both sides with ease and flair. "Why not let the marketplace determine who uses one professional over another? Why not advertise, solicit, use salesmen to tout your service or product? If I can go out and corral a client by finding him, identifying a problem he may not realize he has, and then solve that problem at a reasonable cost, or even an outrageously high cost—what's wrong with that, doctor? I've got to make money first, in sufficient quantity to keep promises I've made to my creditors. Some day I may be able to pick and choose, to take only certain kinds of cases, the truly meritorious ones, but I think right now that these kinds of cases are mostly done by the fat cats who've already made their money and can afford that kind of charity. They've already done what I'm doing now—which is scrambling for every dollar. You're not one of those people who are sold on your own worth because you graduated and have a title—D.V.M.—are you?"

"Of course not," she said angrily.

"But you are insulated from the real world."

"Crap."

"It's true, Judith. What the hell is your overhead—electricity bill, phone bill, drug purchases, city business tax, state excise tax—"

"I don't know. I don't have to. I don't see what that has to do with—"

"—because you're on salary, an employee, protected from economic reality." I knew I should stop, but I couldn't. "You can afford to make all sorts of judgments, just as long as the paycheck is in your hand every two weeks."

"It wouldn't change how I practice medicine," she shouted. "I don't need to lower my standards—and I wouldn't if I had to."

"You sure sound pompous, Judith," I said, turning into the gravel parking lot. Her white van loomed, ghostly in the dark. The sound of barking sounded from the kennel. "How many vet schools are there in this country—maybe fifteen or sixteen?" She nodded. "Well, there are two or three law schools in each state, except New York and California which each have about twenty. So when you graduated you were guaranteed an income of twenty to forty thousand a year. But what I'm guaranteed is the right to practice law with myself as a client. There are a lot of people right now who are a lot smarter than me—people holding the law degree in one hand and starving because they can't bear to get their hands dirty. I come back to the fact that you're insulated from reality because you've never had to face it."

Maybe I'd gone too far. She dug frantically in her purse, searching for her keys. I could tell she liked to fight and didn't lose very often. "I've got to think about that for a while," she said calmly. "I need time for all that to simmer around."

"Maybe the truth is somewhere in between," I said, extending the verbal olive branch.

"I doubt it," she said, rubbing Prosser's ear. "I think you're wrong." She got out of the car, slammed the door with what I considered to be unnecessary force, and strode to her van. She had a nice ass.

Prosser and I drove home. We'd missed the six o'clock news, but as a result of my way with women, we were in plenty of time for the eleven o'clock report.

Chapter 5

The argument with Judith was still on my mind as I stepped off the elevator on Monday morning. Despite the way I'd sounded, I was always conscious that I'd entered a profession with a potential for helping people. It just seemed to me that there was nothing intrinsically ignoble about making a living while I was doing it. And, too, I continued the argument in my head, the kind of people who would come to me for help weren't always going to be stellar personalities.

Jean was waiting outside the door, a large cardboard box at her feet. She was dressed for work, a tidy skirt and blouse, pearls at her throat. "I'll need a key, Mr. Tomkins," she said. "And help getting this inside."

"What in the world's in there?" I unlocked the door and turned to pick up the box. I couldn't. I pushed it inside, with Jean's help.

"Forms. For just about anything you'll ever do."

"Must be a lot of them."

"Yes. I've spent many years collecting them. Every time I came across a particularly nice one, I'd copy it and bring it home. I knew they'd come in handy some day." She beamed. "And now they have."

Jean looked uncommonly cheerful for one whose dog was languishing in the throes of—whatever that liver ailment was she'd told Judith about. I knew how I'd feel if Prosser had it. I decided to be casual. "How's your Dane coming along, Mrs. Campbell?" I didn't want to get too pushy. Judith had men- **59** tioned that the particular disease was apt to be fatal if left untreated too long. "Did you run him in for tests?"

· She looked up at me from the floor, where she had opened the box and was removing great quantities of paper, sorting them into separate stacks. Her face became a delicate pink. "Mr. Tomkins," she cleared her throat, looked down again at the tidy piles of forms, "I don't have a dog."

"No sick dog?" I said stupidly.

"Nor a well one, either, I'm afraid."

"You mean to tell me all that talk to Judith was about a nonexistent animal?"

"Yes." She rose to her knees. "You see, I needed something to keep a veterinarian on the phone long enough for you to drive to Magnolia. I do a lot of crossword puzzles, you see, and I'd had occasion to look up that word—it's a great word, isn't it?—and all I had to do was feed the symptoms to Dr. Latimer very slowly, one at a time. I think she enjoyed the guessing. Eventually she provided the diagnosis. I hope you don't mind."

"Mind? I think it was terrific. Very resourceful. I was able to get Prosser back and everything." I was beginning to like this lady. I showed her how to disengage the answering service, gave her the numbers of Debi and Virginia so she could call them and tell them the job was taken.

Jean spent the morning making lists on her steno pad of the things she felt we needed. It was nice to have somebody answer the phone, to fend off the people I didn't want to talk to and to be charming to those I did.

Every so often, I'd walk to look over her shoulder. The list kept getting longer, and my unease grew with every stroke of her pen. "Okay, Jean, we're going to have to talk. You're writing down a list of things that look like enough to equip a forty-man firm. True, my practice has picked up—but most of the money I have on hand is from one settlement. I just don't know what's going to be next."

"I can understand that, Mr. Tomkins—"

"Mr. Tomkins is my father. He's in California with my mother. Call me Mike."

"All right, Michael. One of the things I'm going to be doing here is taking care of the books. There are only two things that are indispensable right away, and those are the Xerox machine and some sort of office typewriter. We can get both of them for a reasonably small monthly payment. Any worker needs the proper tools."

"It's entirely possible that your idea of a 'reasonable monthly payment' might be very different than mine."

"I won't do anything except order the typewriter and the Xerox until after I do the first billing. Then I'll have a pretty good idea of what the anticipated cash flow will be for the following—"

"Uh . . . I don't bill people. I mean, I don't do it with pieces of paper at the end of the month or anything. I really think I get better results reminding them when I talk to them on the phone . . ." I stopped talking, cowed by the look of utter disbelief on her face.

"That's the most ridiculous thing I've ever heard. Do you mean to tell me," she strode to the single filing cabinet against the wall and pulled it open, revealing a collection of fifty or sixty mismatched files, "that you actually believe that you can carry the balances for all of your clients in your head, and just happen to be able to bring it up when they happen to call you? And what if they don't call you? What then?"

"It's worked for me for over a year now, and I think it's the best way." I figured she'd worked for the old-time attorneys for so long, perhaps she couldn't really be flexible enough to fit into my scheme of things. I hadn't planned on having my secretary handle any of the money matters at all, come to think of it. I felt it would be better to have my financial dealings private.

I tried to explain. "I've always felt that sometimes attorneys charge people on a scale that has more to do with their overhead than what they actually do for them. My overhead has always been small. I have a personal relationship with each one of my clients, and I think I really do better this way. When I ask them to send me a few bucks—"

"If and when you remember to ask them to send you a few bucks, that's probably exactly what they do." Jean looked disgusted. "How do you manage your trust moneys—or are you so friendly that you take the expenses from your own pocket?"

Stung, I showed her the loose-leaf binder where I'd made a page for each client, showing moneys paid into the trust account and moneys paid out. I hate bookkeeping, and I'm not normally very good at it, but this book I was proud of. "See, it's all here."

"It certainly is," she flipped through the book. "In some cases, you even have money going out when there isn't any money in. Or were you expecting that this client would give you a call in the next day or two?"

Actually, the oversights in that book were significant. The trust account is regulated by the bar association and the rules for its accounting are strict. Most cases require the expenditure of some sort of money—for filing fees, for process service, for all the little procedural things that need doing and cost fifteen dollars here, fifty dollars there. Each client's account should be kept separate—by law.

"What I'm going to do, Michael is this: I will go down to the bank today and open two new accounts. One will be an office account, into which I will deposit each month enough to pay the running expenses around here. The other will be a general account. Anything over and above those expenses will be paid from that account to you." She grabbed her purse. "In fact, I'm going to do that right now. All right?"

"Sounds okay to me," I said softly, as the door swung shut behind her. I was beginning to understand that Jean fully intended to take over the office side of the practice without any interference from me. As the months went by, I was to become grateful for that fact. But now, as I examined the forms stacked tidily around the large cardboard box, I reluctantly let go of my technicolor dream of myself, wise and patient, instructing a tender young thing in the intricacies of trilling good morning and giving me my messages.

Obviously, Jean needed no such instruction. And just as obviously she'd not learned her trade from watching old movies, either.

I was already at the point of being busy most hours of a normal working week. One referral had led to another, and my office began to take on the semblance of a real lawyer's workplace. Jean was able to shield me from the callers to whom I didn't want to speak, in the process displaying a talent for dissembling that matched the story she'd told Judith about her nonexistent dog.

One morning Jean dropped a book on my desk. "Lawyer referral is sending over a couple to see you this afternoon. Their name is Peavey, and they should be here at one. The problem is some sort of landlord-tenant dispute involving a twenty-day notice. I spoke to Mr. Peavey on the phone, and he was rather inarticulate, but he was served with a Summons and Complaint yesterday. So," she indicated the book, "I borrowed this from upstairs so you can be familiar with the terms and so forth. Sort of refresh your mind."

I spent the next hour reading the Landlord-Tenant Act. There are several ways a tenant can be evicted. A twenty-day notice can be served on a tenant for any reason at all when a landlord wishes the tenancy terminated. There are some reasons that are unlawful, such as discrimination by race, creed, or color. The tenant has the same option to terminate the tenancy upon twenty-days' notice.

One interesting thing about eviction lawsuits, called "unlawful detainer actions," is that these actions are one of the few for which the court can order attorney's fees to be paid to the prevailing party. Interesting.

"Mr. Peavey is here," Jean slipped into my office, pulling the door closed behind her. "And Mrs. Peavey is with him."

She held her arms in front of her belly, pantomiming advanced pregnancy. "We'll have to bring my chair in here," she said, "since Mr. Peavey has taken the only waiting-room chair without seeming to care whether or not she stands."

"You don't like him."

"I didn't say that, Michael. It's too early to tell. I'll bring them in."

Mr. Peavey—Gil—was a tall man in his late twenties, with a head of curly red hair and a full beard. He shook my hand vigorously. He did indeed appropriate the one chair, not seeming to notice Jean's struggle to bring the desk chair inside for his wife.

Julie Peavey was pale to the point of disappearing. The entire time they spent in my office, she said not one word. Gil did enough talking for both of them, anyway.

He passed me a Summons and Complaint which was stained with some sort of goo that resembled strained peas. I hoped it was strained peas, and not something worse. "Some dude gave this to Julie last night," he said, rocking back in the chair.

"This is a Summons and Complaint for Unlawful Detainer," I said.

"Hey, man. That's brilliant. Just what it says at the top. I know what it is—but I also know we got rights. He don't fix the heat, we don't pay the rent." He let the chair slam to the floor.

"You were served with the twenty-day notice to vacate just about three weeks ago?" I began taking notes.

"Uh-huh. Right after I called the health inspector. That landlord don't want no troublemakers around his dump, that's for sure."

"The reason he wants you to leave is because you complained about the lack of heat?" That was a possible defense. I wrote it down. "Who did you talk to at the Health Department? Did they come out and investigate?"

Gil waved his hand. "We have all that stuff written down at

home. He says we're behind in the rent, too—but I know my rights. He has to provide us with heat, or we don't have to pay the rent, right?"

It wasn't quite that simple, but I nodded. "Can you think of any other reason why your landlord might want you to vacate?"

"Probably so he can rent out that dump to some people stupider than us, right?" Gil leaned forward. I noticed when his shirt fell away from his chest that he had a gaudy tattoo that appeared large enough to extend down over his stomach. "Seems like you can't get ahead if you're a plain working stiff. The landlords'll find a way to stick it to you. Right, Julie?"

Julie nodded, hands folded across her enormous belly.

"Okay. I'll call the attorney on the other side and see if we can work something out. At least get the heat turned on, get you a little caught up on your rent. If I can't work something out, maybe we'll have to set a trial date. I'll call you and let you know what's going to happen.

I could imagine the situation. The rapacious landlord—slumlord, really—not bothering to maintain his units, demanding ever-increasing rent payments, not willing to give these young people time to get back on their feet.

"Is fifty enough to get you started?" Gil extended some folded bills. "It's all I can do right at the moment, man —but next week when the unemployment comes in, I can give you more. What do you think this is going to cost?"

"I'll know more tomorrow, after I've talked to the other attorney," I said, taking the money. "It's possible, if we have to go to trial, that I can get attorney's fees included in the judgment."

Gil nodded his head toward the door. Julie stood obediently. "That's great, man. Later."

I handed Jean the money after she'd shown them out. "Here. I think we might end up going to trial on this one."

"Did you discuss fee with them, other than this?" Jean held

the money with her fingertips. "Do you think they can afford you?"

"Jean," I said patiently, "I'm in business to take every case that comes through the door. I'm not going to turn down—"

"I should think you'd be in business to take every *paying* case that comes through the door. A fine distinction, Michael, but an important one."

"The landlord's trying to get them out. They're troublemakers—they called the authorities to complain about a broken heater. They have kids, Jean—and no heat."

"Be careful, Michael. There may be more to it than that."

"You should have a little more confidence in me than that, Jean. I'm going to call the other attorney right now, then I'll know more."

John Simpson, the attorney for the landlord, was not amenable to any discussion of the matter whatsoever. "We'll see you in court," he said.

I called Gil the following morning. "We're going to have to go to trial," I told him. "But I can stall and get you more time."

"Hey, man, that's great. The unemployment hasn't been extended, but I'm pretty sure I'm going to be called back to work any day now. If I can just get a few weeks clear, I can pay the back rent and your fee easy."

I asked that he send me all the documents pertaining to the rental of the apartment, any documentation of the conversation with the health inspector, any cancelled rent checks—all things I'd like to have by time of trial.

The landlord couldn't go ahead and have the Peaveys evicted until the trial was over. Sometimes, I thought, all people needed was a little breathing space. The Peaveys were trying to raise a family in an economy that was uncertain at best. I only had Prosser to feed, and that was responsibility enough. I wondered how I'd handle it if I were in Gil Peavey's place, with a handful of kids already and another on the way. And no job.

"It seems to me that if I had all those children, I'd find a job—any job," said Jean sourly.

"You don't like him, do you?"

"No, I don't. But that has nothing to do with why I don't think you should have taken his case. That was a strictly business evaluation. I don't think you're going to get paid."

"But attorney's fees can be awarded in unlawful detainer actions," I said. "So it looks pretty good."

"That's if you win."

"True. But landlords have a reputation for victimizing people who don't know any better. I imagine he has a lot of units and cuts corners all the time. Even if he comes across one once in a while who fights back, it's still pretty profitable."

"I wonder if it's that simple," Jean shrugged. "Here are your messages. I've arranged these in order of importance."

"Judith Latimer called?" That one was right on top.

"Yes. She's a charming girl. Lovely manners."

"Did she say why she called?"

"Prosser has to have his leg checked one more time. She said you knew about it."

I did. But I'd been waiting to call until I could clarify for myself exactly why I felt the way I did about my profession. I had a hunch that until I stopped flipping from one opinion to the other, I'd continue to make a fool of myself with Judith.

Now was an excellent time to call. Not only was I making a living, but I was doing good, too. It wasn't that I was astride the white horse, exactly, but helping the Peavey family get a fresh start after a run of bad luck would be the sort of thing I could relate to Judith without risking her scorn, as my Edna story had.

"Doctor Latimer." Her voice was clipped, professional. I could hear a cacophony of barking.

"This is Lawyer Tomkins. I'd like to have you take a look at

Prosser's leg. Actually, it looks better now since you fixed it than before the accident."

"Mike! I'm glad you called. I wasn't sure I'd hear from you again after—"

"Yeah. I wasn't as positive about everything as I sounded, you know."

"I guess I wasn't either."

"Do you need to see Prosser's leg at the clinic? Because if you don't, why don't you meet me downtown for dinner and then we can go out to my place and you can take a look at Prosser. How's that for a 'come up and see my etchings' line?"

"Well . . . I usually like to look at the animals here. Has he been favoring it at all? Any limping or any biting at it, things like that?"

"No. It doesn't seem to bother him at all."

"Okay. I'll meet you."

Judith threw back her head and laughed. She had a full-throated laugh. "He sounds like a rude person, your Gil Peavey—and where did he get a name like that?"

"He is rude. Jean disliked him on sight."

"Jean impressed me as somebody whose snap judgments would be accurate most of the time."

"She's worried that he won't pay me."

"Maybe he won't."

"Did I tell you about his tattoo?" I described him with a full-blown description of the tattoo, embellishing liberally. It was good to see Judith smile, especially at me.

Prosser was glad to see her again. He was a perfect host, dropping his soggy bear in her lap, sitting like a gentleman while she inspected it. "I like your toy, Prosser," she said. "What is it?" she asked me, sotto voce.

I was favorably impressed with her delicacy.

She examined Prosser's leg, pronouncing him cured. We toasted his recovery with a fine bottle of burgundy I'd been saving for a special occasion, pouring Prosser a small tot in a saucer.

He sniffed it inquisitively, backed away, sat down. Sniffed again, took a tentative slurp. His tail, thick and plumy now that he was grown, belying the scruffy appearance it had had during his puppyhood, waved slowly. He slurped again, turning his massive head to eye us appreciatively.

"We shouldn't really be giving him that stuff," said Judith. "It's not good for him, you know."

"Can't you ever relax? It isn't good for us, either."

"Sorry." She knelt to pet Prosser, who had collapsed with a groan on the floor "I think he's a magnificent dog."

"Yeah, he is." I told her about our early days, the partnership of Prosser and Tomkins, our client-getting forays throughout the city.

"I love that story," she said. "I think it's more difficult now for you to make him a part of your life."

"Yeah, I guess it is. But I still bring him to work with me sometimes. He's well behaved and doesn't commit any indiscretions. I think he means so much to me because when I came to this city, I didn't know a soul, and he's always been excellent company."

"Mm-hmmm. I remember how good an animal's company can be. When I was a little girl, I had a boxer—a brindle named Ginger. But I called her Moose. I loved that dog so much. She died when I was about fourteen—of old age, I guess. If there was ever a moment when I decided, really decided what I was going to do with my life, it was when Ginger died."

"I didn't have any pets when I was a kid."

"Nothing? Not even a goldfish?" She pretended amazement. "Not even a mealworm or a cockroach?"

"Not a thing. Prosser is the only pet I've ever had." I poured us some more wine.

"What kind of a kid were you, Mike?"

"My childhood is something I'd rather forget. At least the

early part of it. I didn't seem to fit in anywhere. I couldn't read—"

"Why not?"

Nobody knew, at first. My first-grade teacher encouraged my parents to put me in a school for the functionally retarded. I stuttered, the whole bit."

"What did your parents do about it?"

"Beat me. No—everything they could. In those days, special learning disability hadn't really been discovered yet . . ." As I told Judith about those early school years, I remembered the fear and pain as though it had happened that week.

In kindergarten, I suspected as much, but by the time I hit first grade, I was certain: I was far, far too stupid ever to learn anything. This attitude was enthusiastically encouraged by my teacher, Mrs. Robbins, who ran the class with a degree of flexibility and tenderness appropriate to Devil's Island.

I don't think she really gave a damn whether or not I ever learned to read, but the stuttering really got to her. "You can stand here until you get it right, Michael," she'd say, usually just before recess. I'd stand alone in the deserted classroom, stammering endlessly to say one sentence, just one sentence correctly.

"Do you have it yet?" Mrs. Robbins would ask, as the whole class trooped in after recess.

I'd shake my head miserably, holding back the tears.

"Well, try. We'd all be interested in hearing you try, Michael."

So I'd try, "W-w-we can have f-f-flowers—"

"That's sufficient, Michael."

And it was. I went off to school each day with a fear inside too large to share with anyone, even my parents. There were compensations, though. I had my magic. Alone in my room, I could make the scarf change color, make the pennies disappear.

And there, with my imaginary audience of thousands, I

was articulate. I didn't stammer, I didn't stutter—the magic patter came out without a hitch. I was the consummate magician, with hands faster than anyone's eye. Even Mrs. Robbins's.

When I was picked to present something to the class for show-and-tell on Monday, I knew just what it would be.

My big brother had given me a new trick for Christmas—a disappearing egg trick. There was a cunningly designed wooden box, lined in rich purple velvet. I had practiced again and again placing an egg in the box, closing the tiny hinged lid. "And now, ladies and gentlemen, I pass my hands once, twice, three times over the box, and . . ." I'd lift the lid, displaying only the smooth purple velvet. For a magician such as myself, making the egg disappear was easy. I'd bring down the house, make them all love me. Even her.

I didn't sleep well Sunday night, and was up early Monday morning, packing and repacking my trick. The box was wrapped carefully in flannel, tucked inside a shopping bag. The egg was nestled securely in a cut-out part of a carton. Show-and-tell was the first thing on Monday's schedule.

"Michael, what are you going to show us this morning?"

"My hobby—magic."

"Oh."

"Okay?"

"Well, if that's your hobby . . ."

I rose, a little nervous, but eager to astound them all. It went well, at first. My audience was rapt and wide-eyed as I passed the little box around for all to examine, secure in the thought that its mysteries were hidden to all but magicians. When everyone had had a chance to examine it, I produced the egg. "An ordinary egg," I told them, holding it aloft for inspection. "I will place it in the box." I closed the box, covered it with the flannel.

"And now, ladies and gentlemen, before your very eyes, I'm g-g-going to make this egg d-d-disappear, so—"

"Mike," Mrs. Robbins said, "you stuttered just now. So why

don't you slow down a little and start over. That way we can all understand you. It isn't fair to the class if we can't."

"B-b-but—"

"See? Start over now."

I took a deep breath. "And n-n-now, ladies and gentlemen, I'm g-g-going—"

"Mike, start over. You're not trying. Is he, class?" Twenty heads shook from side to side. "See? Now start over."

"I was almost d-d-done. C-c-can't I—"

"From the beginning. *Please*," she said sternly.

One more time. I made it through the intro, but couldn't quite manage *h-h-hands*.

"Over again, Mike. We will all wait until you stop that stuttering, even if it takes all morning—won't we, class?" Twenty heads nodded.

The tears came. I tried to still the trembling of my lips, tried to blink enough times so that I could see the room again. "I can't do it," I yelled. "I just can't—I'm not doing it on purpose—I just c-c-can't—"

"Well, class, I don't know what we're going to do with—"

Frightened she would make me do my outburst over again, too, I bolted for the door. Ignoring Mrs. Robbins's commands to stop, I ran down the polished linoleum hall, out the front door, and all the way home. I don't do magic any more.

"You know," Judith's voice was low, "I think cruelty to anything or anybody that can't fight back is just about the worst thing there is."

I couldn't speak. Every time I remembered that incident, the panic closed my throat just as it did that day when I was six. I hadn't told many people about it, and now that I'd told Judith, I was feeling the way you feel when you've extended some inside part of yourself to another. A little tentative, a little afraid.

Judith moved closer, touched my knee. "Your brother must have loved you a lot, giving you that very special trick, I mean."

"Yeah. He was terrific. A great brother. He's not like me. I mean, not now, when we're all grown up. He's serious and studious—and brilliant."

"Does he still tune into your strengths, and not your weaknesses?"

Actually, I'd never thought about Richard like that before. "I guess he does."

"That's nice," said Judith dreamily. "And now you can do the same for him."

"That's the weird thing about Richard—his weaknesses *are* his strengths." I stroked her hair. It was softer than it looked to be, and was gathered in a loose knot at her nape. "I think I've done enough talking about myself for one night. Let's talk about you."

"There'll be time for that," she said, eyes closed. "We'll have lots of time."

I stroked the strong line of her eyebrows. "I think you're right."

"Michael," said Jean one morning as the trial date for the Peaveys was approaching fast, "your Mr. Peavey hasn't sent any documentation for you to have on hand for the trial. And there isn't much time left. Perhaps you ought to give him a call and remind him. And perhaps," she said maliciously, "you might ask him to send you a few bucks while he's at it."

She was right. The trial was only four days away, and the documents weren't in yet, nor had I received another dime from "my Mr. Peavey." I called him.

"Hi, Mike. How you doing?" Gil sounded like he'd been asleep. "Yeah, yeah. I'm getting those things off to you today—or maybe I'll have Julie run over with them. You know how it goes when you're a family man, a million things to keep track of."

I asked him if he'd returned to work yet, trying to be delicate about broaching the subject of money.

"Not yet, not yet," he told me heartily. "But soon. The foreman says we're going to be called back any day now."

I'd managed to delay the trial so that the end result to the Peaveys was sixty-eight days more than we'd had originally. "Okay, I'd like you to meet me at the courthouse fifteen or twenty minutes early so we can go over your testimony, okay?"

"Sure. Do you want me to bring Julie, too?"

"When's the baby due?"

"Any minute."

"Yeah, if she's still walking around, bring her." It couldn't hurt.

"Hey, Mike. Let me give you a good tip for Longacres. Bart's Brother in the fifth. That horse is a hell of a good mudder."

"Mother?" I asked, not certain I was hearing correctly.

"No, mudder. He's good on a wet track. And don't forget where you heard it."

Not likely. "See you on Thursday."

"Right."

Jean walked in. "I take it he isn't going to send you any money, and I bet you don't get any documents, either."

"You're such a betting woman, Jean—let me give you a tip. Bart's Brother in the fifth. He's a mudder."

On Thursday, I walked into the courtroom at five after nine, twenty-five minutes before we were to begin. The Peaveys hadn't arrived yet. At the counsel table, John Simpson, attorney for the landlord was already there, papers spread on the table before him. "I hope this isn't going to take very long, Mike," he said as I walked toward the left side of the L-shaped table. "I have to be in federal court for a hearing at eleven."

"It shouldn't take long, John. You know my case. I'm putting Gil and Julie Peavey on."

"Do you really think they'll be here this morning?" The man sitting alongside Simpson didn't look like my idea of a slumlord. He was neatly dressed, stocky, with a florid face. He may have been fifty, with neatly barbered iron-gray hair. "I don't think they're going to show," he said.

"Have we met?" I asked.

Simpson performed the introduction. The man was Jim Wilson, the owner of the building where the Peaveys lived.

"I spoke to Mr. Peavey two days ago," I told him. "They'll be here. As you know, Julie was about to have her baby, and—"

"Nonsense." Mr. Wilson shook his head. "I own those four units. If you could see the damage that has been done within the past thirty-six hours to that place, you'd be as certain as I am that they have no intention of showing up."

"What the hell are you talking about?"

Simpson pulled out a stack of Polaroid color photographs from his briefcase. "I'm sorry, Mike."

I felt absurdly young and inexperienced, and even began to blush as I examined the pictures. "Their unit?" I asked in a small voice, even though I knew it was.

The pictures showed an apartment that had been trashed—systematically trashed, from the look of it. Garbage was all over, holes were kicked in every wall, windows splintered. The interior doors hung from broken hinges, ceiling fixtures were missing, ripped out. "When did they leave?"

Mr. Wilson rubbed his forehead wearily. "My manager said they pulled out sometime Monday night or Tuesday morning."

The bailiff appeared, asking us to rise. The judge paced the two steps to his black leather chair. "All parties ready?"

"Plaintiff is ready, your Honor."

I stood, a little shakily. "Uh, your Honor, my clients, Mr. and Mrs. Peavey, have not arrived as of yet. I have no reason to believe they're not coming."

The judge glanced at the clock. "We will wait until 9:50, Mr. Tomkins. Then we will proceed."

"Thank you, your Honor."

We stood as the judge left the bench. I paced the hall, eyeing the elevator every time it appeared. It disgorged an array of people, none of whom was either one of the Peaveys.

At 9:50 the judge came back to the bench. I watched as Simpson put Wilson on the stand, led him through his paces. Yes, the notices were properly served, more than twenty days had elapsed, rent was overdue, waste was committed upon the premises.

In all cases, the plaintiff must affirmatively prove his case, even though the defendants will not present testimony.

All requirements were met, and Mr. Wilson took a judgment against the Peaveys for $790 back rent, attorney's fees in an amount of $400, and costs of suit in the amount of $74. A total judgment of $1,264, which was going to be uncollectible. Everyone knew that.

The whole procedure took fifteen minutes. Simpson clicked his briefcase shut, stood up, and with a wave to Wilson and myself sauntered to the door. Wilson remained at the table, as if he wanted to talk to me. "Mr. Tomkins, may I have a moment of your time?"

I didn't want to talk to him. "Sure," I said dully. "But please, call me Mike."

"I just wanted to tell you," he spoke quietly, "that my loss on this fiasco is going to be close to forty-five hundred dollars. You don't make the laws, I realize that, but," his voice rose, "as an officer of the court and a decent human being—well, I just think that you've got one hell of a nerve. Stalling, keeping me from making my payments on time— did you ever think of that? For what?" He faced me, palms up and outspread on the glossy table. "Can you tell me for what?"

How could I explain to this man that doing good wasn't always what it appeared to be, and that I'd done the wrong thing, not from malicious intent, but from stupidity and lack of experience?

"You know," he continued, his voice soft once again, "a man with a briefcase can do a hell of a lot more damage, sometimes, than a man with a gun. You've affected a lot of lives, here, Mike."

"I'd like to explain—"

He waved that away. "It doesn't do any good now. You know, my son—my oldest boy—he's a senior at U.C.L.A. He's always said he wants to be a lawyer, and I was proud of him. Proud. But now, I don't know. I think you'd better give the cases you take and the way that you handle them a good deal more thought than you did this time. Mr. Simpson tells me you're a good lawyer, doing right by your clients and all. And I wouldn't have minded a fair hearing at the beginning. But the delays, Mike, the delays. Where's the justice in that?"

I was shook up. I was humiliated, and I wanted this man to know that it wasn't like he thought. But it was, of course. More than that, I wanted him to understand why I did what I did. I wanted to say I'm sorry. But it didn't seem like a professional thing to do.

"Mr. Wilson, let me tell you just how good a lawyer I am. I lost my ass on this case. I got stiffed by that bastard because I believed him, I bought the whole package. Who one believes and when—well, it's not always that easy. I feel terrible about this. I'm sorry about your money."

Mr. Wilson nodded. "Call me Jim, Mike. And enough apology. You're young yet—you have a lot to learn. But you're willing to listen and to admit it when you make a mistake. In my book, that's a fine thing. Come on, I'll buy you an orange juice to wash down the humble pie."

Over juice in the cafeteria, he told me insurance would cover most of the repairs to the apartment. In addition, he told me I drank too much orange juice and should listen to my secretary.

I told Jean the whole story. "It's one hell of an expensive way to learn a lesson," I finished miserably.

"Not so, Michael. Despite what you rather melodramatically told Mr. Wilson, the only thing you lost on this was some time. And at your age, you have plenty of that. Come on, I'll take you to lunch."

"Jean, I don't think you could afford to take Tinkerbell to lunch on what I pay you."

"Correct, Michael," she said, taking my arm, "but I had a modest run of success at the track Saturday. Bart's Brother in the fifth. That horse is one hell of a mudder."

It wasn't long after that that Mr. Wilson called me and invited me to have lunch with him.

"I can't imagine why," I told Jean. "Maybe he has a problem and needs help—but, then, why wouldn't he get Simpson?"

"Maybe he can't afford Simpson any more, since he lost so badly on the Peavey eviction," she said.

"Actually, Mike, I don't have a problem at all," said Mr. Wilson. "But I am presented with a situation which could turn out to be a good thing for both of us."

Jim Wilson was the subrogation manager for Cascade Insurance Company. When an insured person becomes involved in an accident with another party, the insurance company turns to the other party or his insurance company for repayment of that loss. In the event that there is an opposing insurance company involved, the matter is often settled by arbitration. If the other party is uninsured, the paying insurance company looks directly to that individual for repayment.

"Our company is taking an aggressive posture on these things, Mike. It's a quantity operation—right now maybe twenty to thirty cases a month. After that, who knows? Simpson doesn't want to handle this sort of thing, since they are time-consuming—but then I thought of you."

I resisted an impulse to kiss his hand. "Is there some procedure you have for collecting these things, or—"

"No. That would be totally up to you. We ask that you keep us informed of developments, of course. In the event that you collect, forty percent of the money is yours. You pay expenses." He signaled for the check. "I assume your office could be set up to handle something like this?"

I thought of Jean at her little desk, our one filing cabinet. "Of course we are. Anything I couldn't handle personally could be handled by my associates." Or my cast of thousands. I was suddenly thankful that I'd decided to meet Jim Wilson at the restaurant, sparing him a view of my expensively furnished downtown office.

"Well, think it over, Mike. Could you let me know by the end of the week? I'm getting a lot of pressure to send these cases out for action right away."

"Could I let you know right now? I'll do it," I said. "But why me?"

"I need somebody I can work with, and I think you'll be willing to learn," said Wilson.

"It's a good thing you didn't appear too eager," said Jean after I'd told her the whole story. "I think we can handle it—for the first month or two, anyway. But, Michael, if that's true—twenty to thirty cases a month—we're soon going to have to streamline operations around here a bit more."

"I don't know why we couldn't handle it ourselves," I said grandly.

"It seems to me," Jean said, "that an insurance company wouldn't send something to an outside attorney unless they'd tried everything they know to pry some money loose. Eventually, I suppose, it'll settle down to a percentage—so many are possibles, and the rest are just dead."

"Does this bode well?" I asked her, grinning from ear to ear.

"Can't hurt. I'm proud of you, Michael. You turned a debacle into an opportunity and now we'll have to see just how good a secretary I am."

"You handle the paper work," I told her expansively, "and if you're really good I'll buy you a rubber thumb."

Chapter 6

"Michael, it's somebody who won't give his name—or at least won't give his *real* name. Long distance, from the sound of it." Even over the new intercom, Jean's voice sounded disapproving. People who played guessing games on the telephone were the bane of her existence. "He says to tell you it's 'Chops.' "

"John Lamb!" I cried excitedly. Even though I pushed the off button on the intercom, I could still hear Jean's exasperated snort. "John? You been disbarred yet?"

"How you doing, Mike? Chasing ambulances in all that Seattle rain couldn't be good for your health."

"So how are things in frigid Minneapolis?"

"I wouldn't know. I'm in D.C. American Bar Association project on Rules for Civil Procedure." His voice capitalized the initial letters.

"Sounds right up your alley—"

"Yeah. I never minded research, as you know. It's kind of fun. Meeting with local bar association types, judges, that sort of thing. Lots of travel."

"So your cheating in law school paid off."

"Was that a real person who answered the phone and interrogated me? Didn't sound like an answering service."

"I have a secretary now." I lowered my voice. "An old broad, but a hard worker and she knows a lot—"

"What are you paying her with? Don't tell me you're making money."

"Some. I can compete with her Medicare and Social Security, anyway."

"So you must be doing okay. Last time I talked to you—God, it must be better than a year and a half ago, right? I was still in Minneapolis looking around for something else and you were in Seattle looking for something to eat."

"I got lucky." It was so good to hear John's voice again. We'd met in law school—roomed together, in fact. He was tall and rosy-cheeked. We were opposites in looks and in temperament, but the rooming arrangement worked, and so did our friendship. He was tidy and methodical—even had creases ironed into his jeans. It used to take him more than an hour to go out in the morning, even if all he was doing was going to class. He'd shower, shave, slap his cheeks to a rosier glow, polish his shoes.

We'd talk about the future—what we'd be doing in five years, in ten years. Boy, we'd talked—where we'd practice, what kind of law, how many secretaries and associates, and in John's case, how soon he'd be made partner. We both assumed that he'd have no trouble getting into one of the bigger law firms and being suitably rewarded for his diligence. He really *liked* research.

"You must have gotten lucky if you can afford a secretary and a phone with more than one line."

"Yeah. It's been a good year. I got so excited after I did the books. After paying the bills I had enough left over to buy a color TV. I've arrived, John. Did you know that the stuff they play football on is green?"

"Okay, Mike, since you're doing so well, I'm sure you can afford to pay for this call, even if it was your nickel, which it isn't. But I'm not in private practice so I've got to get back to work. I'm coming to Seattle later this week. Can you put me up?"

"Put you up? I'll kill a fatted calf. I'll pick you up at the airport." I took his flight information, grinning from ear to ear. "Is this trip business or pleasure?"

"Business. Some stuff to do at a judicial conference there. But I'm interviewing at a few firms while I'm in town. I'll tell you all about it when I get there."

"You know who that was?" I asked Jean, straddling the tiny visitor's chair in front of her desk.

"No, I certainly do not, since he wouldn't give me his name," she said, peering over her glasses at me.

"He wanted to surprise me, Jean. If he'd told you who he was, it wouldn't have been a surprise, would it?"

She smiled. "I can keep a secret, you know." She removed her glasses, turned off the typewriter, and folded her hands on the desk. "Well, tell me."

"John Lamb, my friend from law school. He's flying in on Wednesday; he'll be staying with me for a while."

"You're so excited—he must be a good friend."

"Yeah. Like a brother, in fact. I know that sounds corny, but that's the way it was."

"So, when will he be here?"

"Some time in the afternoon."

"We'll be ready for him." She turned back to the typewriter, the new IBM. "We should get the maintenance crew in here to mop up the floor. And maybe you and I can make an appointment for after he leaves—to talk about new office space."

"New space?"

"Sure. It's a good time to think about it, because I'd have to order letterheads soon, and it makes sense to wait and get a permanent address. Don't you think that's sensible?"

"But can we afford it?"

"Soon. Very soon."

It struck me, as I returned to my own office, that never in my wildest fantasies had I envisioned myself asking my secretary whether or not we could afford anything. But Jean had indeed moved into the financial side of my life with the same lack of reluctance with which she'd moved into the office side. She simply took over.

It wasn't that she ever did anything with which I disagreed, exactly. She just made it very uncomfortable for me to continue to disagree with something she considered necessary. The billing, for instance. After that first day, she'd let it be for about a month. Then the campaign began.

"Good heavens," she'd said, after pulling one or another of the ledger cards. "Here I see you've never gotten one dime from Joe Smith. And after you spent all that time on him, too."

"Jean," I'd say, resenting the discussion, "I think the way I do it works better, really I do."

"I've heard the way you do it, Michael. You call somebody up *after* you've done the work, when the time you've put into it seems like an awful lot. Then you feel terrible about asking for an honest hourly sum, so you suggest that they 'send you some money.' "

"It works pretty well, too—usually," I said, glaring at her. If my informal billing system hadn't been effective, how did she think I'd been able to hire her? "I think it alienates people to get a bill. I want my clients to know that I'm not any smarter or better than they are, that I'm just a person. If I call them, it's more personal. I think they respond better."

"Nonsense."

"Listen, Jean. It works. I know that. And as long as it works, why change it?"

"I don't believe that it works as well as billing would. And another thing: You can't possibly remember what you told them. You never write anything down. And what if they don't pay? What if it takes three or four months?"

"It would take three or four months anyhow, right? And it's not as if there are too many clients for me to remember. Except," I said, catching myself in time, "for Joe Smith. Somehow that one slipped through the cracks."

"Yes. And he's probably waiting for a bill so he knows how much he owes you." She scribbled something on her note pad. "I'm going to call the printer in the morning and order statement forms." Noticing my mutinous look, she softened. "We'll try it for a few months and see how it goes."

So we did. For a while there, the sight of the little billing envelopes going out once a month made me feel silly—as if I was taking myself too seriously. When I mentioned this to Jean, she said, "That's your biggest problem, Michael, you don't take yourself seriously enough."

I'm still not sure if the billing itself made all that much difference. Maybe it did. I know that sometimes when I'd see the mail, there would be checks from clients I'd thought didn't owe me money, or clients I'd forgotten about. And in a remarkably short time, since Jean billed out things I'd previously handled with a phone call, there were indeed too many accounts for me to remember.

In spite of the fact that the office was tiny and shabby and (Jean was right) the floor was filthy, I was doing better than I had anticipated. I couldn't wait to see John and have a laugh about old times.

"Welcome!" I said heartily, throwing open the door of my little house. Prosser bounded forward, trying to look as if he'd been guarding the color TV from burglars instead of sleeping on the couch.

John swung his suitcase in front of his knees, using it as a shield against Prosser's advances. "God, Tomkins, where'd you get the beast?"

"At the beast store, where else? Prosser, *down*." I grabbed his collar and pulled him away from John's leg. "He's heard so much about you, he feels like he knows you already. He's friendly, you don't have to worry."

John put his suitcase against the wall and gingerly extended a hand to Prosser, who lovingly slurped it.

"Just make yourself at home, John. Have a seat, I'll get you a towel." I knew he wouldn't be able to bring himself to wipe his hands on his pants.

We got reacquainted over gin and tonics. "So how is the job situation here?" John asked, discreetly removing Prosser's jowls from his lap.

"Great, great," I said. "I myself have had more than eleven offers, ranging from lawn work to short-order cook."

"Not good, huh?"

"Well, not for me. But you're probably a better interviewer than me. I always drool on my rep tie."

"We'll see."

"Why are you even thinking about this kind of change? I thought you were happy with your job—"

"Christ, Mike, it's living from one grant to another. This one runs out in four months. I'd like to settle down, do some real lawyering for a change. I'd like to go to court once in a while, maybe do some trial work."

"I never thought I'd live to see the day when you'd consider private practice, John."

He yawned. "I'm beat from the flight. I'm going to turn in. I'm going to use your office number for messages, okay?"

Since we'd gotten the Cascade cases, which did number twenty to thirty a month, Jean and I had been far busier than we'd dreamed we would be. Each of the cases was a lawsuit, and as Jean said, we were at the point of having a small tree's worth of paper pass through the office each day.

Because things had been going well to begin with, one referral often leading to another, I was beginning to share the successful attorney's feelings that when I left the office, I lost money. There was no help for it, though—court appearances were required for many of those suits. I had taken to paying a modest hourly wage to a couple of young lawyers I knew who were looking for work and taking anything they could get in the meantime.

It didn't save me from all the court appearances, but it was a help. The waiting was the factor it was impossible to predict, and increasingly difficult to work around. Sometimes the wait for a thirty-minute case to be called could be as long as forty-five minutes.

Jean and I were developing a number of scheduling problems. For instance, when I put in a notice of appearance on a drunk-driving case, I would be assigned a trial date and notified by mail. If that date was in conflict with something already scheduled, I would have to appear physically in court and wait until the judge had a free moment to sign a continuance. That sort of wasted time is not the kind of thing you can charge a client for—or at least I've never felt right about charging for it. Incredible as it sounds, by being a little too busy, I was losing money.

It seemed to me it was time to sit down with Jean and the books and calculate just how much it was costing me per hour to practice, and how to make the whole operation more efficient.

"Maybe it's time to bring somebody else in, Michael," said Jean. "A young lawyer just starting out, say. Or even John Lamb."

"I can't afford to pay a salary, now—so I really couldn't afford a young lawyer. And John—you don't understand, Jean. John isn't some young kid. He's going to get on at one of the best firms in town, wait and see."

"I haven't noticed that many calls coming in for him," she said. "And I understand it's a bad time for a lawyer to be looking for work—there are so many of you now."

"But John's good. He'll be able to get on anywhere."

"I think the fact that he's been working for all those agencies for five years might be a drawback, rather than an advantage," Jean said.

"How do you figure that?"

"Well," she said thoughtfully, "if I were responsible for hiring in a large firm, I'd want to hire new people who were young enough to work for very little while they got experience. He's not had a chance to specialize in anything to the extent that anybody is going to pay him more because of a certain kind of knowledge. He's charming and handsome, and you tell me he's brilliant, but I think he's neither fish nor fowl at this point in his life."

"I don't think it's that bleak," I said, although I was beginning to wonder.

"By the way, John called and reminded you to be home no later than six-thirty tonight. Any later, he said to tell you, and the sauce would be ruined."

John had been staying at my apartment for ten days. He was watching the news when I came home. Prosser bounded up from the corner where he had taken to lying, in deference to John's clothes. Prosser knew when he wasn't wanted, even if he didn't always understand why.

Unlike myself in my job-hunting days, John had appointments to get turned down, whereas I had free-lanced rejection. "Not so good?" I asked.

"I've been received more warmly in other times of my life," he said dryly, removing a platter of some savory-smelling chicken from the oven.

"It's a bad time to be looking for work," I told him. "Maybe it's just going to take a little longer."

"Maybe. These are good organizations. Nice guys, both directors—but they said that they're getting applications from all over the country. There's just no room. Seattle's lawyer population has swelled. Did you know that since 1900 there have been thirteen thousand lawyers admitted to practice law and that nine thousand of them are practicing right now? Or trying to practice, as the case may be."

"You might want to consider private practice," I said casually.

He didn't look at me. "It's an option. From the looks of this kitchen, private practice isn't treating you that well. Did you know that I had to go out to buy salt for God's sake? All you had in here was fifty pounds of dog food and one desiccated artichoke."

Although we talked about other things, all through dinner the thought stayed in my mind. I didn't need somebody full time, and it had never occurred to me that Lamb might condescend to want to practice with me. But he could take care of my overflow, thus earning enough to eat on for a while, and build his own practice at the same time.

I thought it over until we moved to the living room with our glasses of brandy. "Now, John, maybe we should talk about my future—which until a short while ago, did not include you."

"I'm flattered, Tomkins."

"Don't mention it. I've been looking at the books trying to determine if I could ask the question I'll get around to asking—"

"Perhaps you could get to the point, Tomkins, before I get old?"

"Okay." I took a deep breath. "I'm busy. I'm taking on a lot of chippy little cases that I'm too greedy or too insecure to turn down. It isn't big money, that's for sure—but it's enough work to keep me and Jean busy. Pieces of paper you wouldn't believe."

"You're getting more abstruse, rather than less."

"I'll say it then. If you really want to leave the grantsmanship world and live here to mingle with the moneygrubbers, let's share expenses. You help me with the work load, I pay most of the rent and overhead. You do what you're strong in—research, writing briefs, being thorough—and I'll continue to do what I'm good at."

"Bullshit?"

"Correct. It's a gamble, of course, on both our parts. But I don't have any doubts it will work out, given enough time."

"Can you guarantee me enough to live on?"

I rolled my eyes. "There you go, with the regular paycheck mentality. That's what I mean—there are no guarantees. You can be reasonably certain that you'll eat, even if it's franks and beans. But other than that, I'm not guaranteeing a damn thing."

"When did this idea come to mind?"

"Jean and I have been kicking around the idea of moving to a larger office and getting somebody in to help with the overflow for a long time now. She likes you—a fatal flaw— but she does. And Judith likes you too. I think she was amazed to find that you don't eat your peas with a knife, since anybody who'd roomed with me must by definition be a low fellow."

"Are you serious about this?"

"Listen, Lamb. I am now going to teach you about over-head. At first blush, all a lawyer really needs are a desk, a typewriter, and a phone. It's not like that in the real world." I remember Jean and her steno-pad lists the first week I knew her. "You need a secretary or two, file cabinets, messenger service, furniture, dictating equipment, a copy machine. Add it all up, and it's not cheap.

"The question is, are you ready to throw caution to the wind, leave a salaried position with benefits and security and defined duties and hours—to go into private practice and hope the phone rings?"

"Why were you so hesitant to bring it up?"

"I wasn't exactly hesitant. I just thought you might feel the bottom portion of the legal ladder was beneath you. I didn't want you to have to turn me down."

"I'm tired of having to live from one funding period to another. I guess the only way to tell if you're suited to private practice is to try it. To be honest with you, I'm not sure I'd be any good at dealing with stupid people and the trouble they get into. I've always worked on a sort of—"

"Higher plane?"

"I'm not trying to be snide, Tomkins."

"I know that. But the end result of everything you do in any kind of legal work ultimately comes down to people."

"But groups of them, not individuals."

"Yeah, but groups of people tend to get their legal counsel from big groups of lawyers called firms."

"There's no room in your office for another body unless I sit in Jean's lap. And that I refuse to do. She's not what I would have chosen for a front-office gal."

"Jean is going to be a big help to you, wait and see." I said. "And don't worry about the space. We'll find something before you have to leave D.C. for good. When's that—four months or so?"

"You were really going to move anyhow?"

"Yeah. Jean thinks we've outgrown our present location, and it's been nag, nag, nag. When she decides it's time to do something, I get no peace until I decide it's time to do it, too. She thinks we should get new furniture, too. Hell, I've got wood desks, what else does she want?"

"Maybe she'll get a little more professional with two of us in there," he said. "So you mean that when I come back from D.C. we can start this office-sharing arrangement?"

"If I can find something reasonable," I told him.

"Good. I'll be back in a few months and you can teach me how to make money."

"You scramble for it, Lamb, you scramble for it."

"Yeah, I know," he said, a little distastefully. "So we'll be roomies again when I get back?"

"Sure. You can sleep with Prosser until you get a place of your own."

The next week I began looking for office space to fit our requirements. Finding space has developed into an art form. An entire industry is concerned with finding space, negotiating rents, space planning. It's a commission business, similar to selling real estate, but maybe more complicated. I was getting advice from everyone about where to relocate, how to relocate, the costs of relocating, how many square feet per person per week of activity in relation to the negative ions that may pass between the personnel on any given Thursday afternoon.

"Jesus Christ, Jean," I exploded. "Can't we just find a vacant office and if it has two offices and a secretarial space, take it? If it's cheap enough."

"We'll find the right space soon enough, Michael." Jean paused in her perusal of a list of buildings. "It has to be the right space for us."

"I've never moved before. I don't like it. I hate change, getting uprooted. I'm getting an anxiety attack."

"All the more reason we have to find the right place so we don't have to do it again," Jean said calmly.

"It's all happening so fast. Now Lamb is moving out here, I'm supposed to give him work so he can live I'm not old enough to have this kind of responsibility."

"Michael." Jean put down her list. "Before you whip yourself into a froth, let me tell you what a very dear CPA friend of mine once told me. The worst thing that can happen is that you can't pay the rent. Debtors' prisons don't exist any more."

"That does seem like a sensible way to look at it," I conceded. "If I can't pay the rent, I can start over again and make it the next time."

"Right. Now," she picked up the list again, "we need a good address, one that commands respect. A subtle statement pointing out that you're a real attorney in a good part of town and people will have to pay you what you're worth."

"Oh, my God, Jean, I can't afford to pay what it would cost to make that statement. No offense, but you're back in the days of high-button shoes. Nobody cares what the surroundings are. Give the clients access to counsel at a decent price, give them a smiling face, and they don't care if they sit on leather and antiques or naugahyde. Just give them a cheap will. This is the land of plastic food, K-Mart, and optometrists' offices in Sears."

"Trust me, Michael. It matters. Maybe not to the client,

although I'm not so certain about that. But what about the
other attorneys? They're the people who make you money.
You settle cases with other attorneys, bank people, insurance
adjustors. They look at a good address on the letterhead and
it tells them a whole lot. Don't worry, we'll be able to find a
good address, and an adequate building—and still watch our
pennies carefully."

"You going to build us one?"

"Close. Close, indeed. I think I've located one we can look
at."

"I'm not sure I'm ready to hear this."

"I've been in contact with some people I know around
town. A building in Pioneer Square is being renovated. The
owner is behind schedule and the bank which is financing the
project is extremely anxious to get it rented. A good bar-
gainer, Michael, could put together a very nice deal. First
tenant in a building always gets the best terms. Here's the
phone number."

So it was that less than a month later I found myself haul-
ing boxes up twenty-nine steps to the second landing in a
two-story brick building in Pioneer Square. Judith and Jean
laughed and chattered as they ran blithely up and down,
bantered about the placement of pictures and chairs. Easy
for them to be that cheerful, I thought, since they weren't
responsible for the rent.

I had to admit the space was nice—nine hundred square
feet divided into two attorney's offices and one large reception area. Windows looked down onto the square, where
could be seen tourists and office workers eating lunch on
park benches beneath spreading trecs. It was going to be
nice. Maybe.

Chapter 7

*I'*d always said that there were two classes of criminal clients that I'd never represent—rapists and child molesters. With my feelings getting in the way, I reasoned, I wouldn't be able to give them a good defense. With my practice going well— or at least well enough to keep myself in food with enough left to give John the chance to pay his bills, too—I knew that it was a matter of time before I'd have to turn down one or the other.

When the Office of Public Defense called and asked me to see Willy Buford, who had been arrested just that morning for molesting his neighbor's child, I hesitated. "Let me check my calendar," I said, hitting the hold button.

The new offices, decorated carefully by Judith and Jean, were beautiful. It was a nice place to come to work each day. Lamb's office adjoined mine, and through the open door, I could see him busily taking notes from a large leather-bound book. That man certainly did like research. Jean's typing could be heard from the reception area, where we'd placed comfortable easy chairs and a table of magazines for the clients—*Sports Illustrated, Barrister,* and *Mad.*

I could at least *see* the guy, I told myself. Maybe he didn't do it. Anyhow, he's entitled to see a lawyer. Well, hell, just seeing him wouldn't commit me to anything.

The county jail is on the top floor of the courthouse, which was a ten-minute walk away. What would he be like, I wondered, as I found myself entering the double glass doors. A child molester.

The deputy recognized me and punched a button on her console, which gleamed and buzzed behind thick glass. I sat on a hard wooden chair at a place along the table which was bisected by steel bars. I reached into my briefcase and pulled out my pen, a yellow ruled legal pad, and my Travis McGee book. This jail, like all jails and most institutions, is run for incompetents by incompetents. Usually, you'll get to see your client anywhere from five to fifty minutes after he's called down from the holding unit.

I settled in for a read, looking forward to floating the waters of Bahia Mar with Trav and Meyer. As I looked up to turn a page, the door opened and a smallish, middle-aged man peered around the room, blinking.

"Mr. Buford?" I asked.

He sidled over. "Yes, suh."

"Hi." I extended my hand. "I'm Mike Tomkins. I'm going to be your attorney."

He stuck his small damp hand through the bars and shook mine weakly. His fingernails were dirty. The light gray jail jumpsuit was too big for him. The cuffs were rolled up five inches above his ankles.

So far he was everything I had expected. He sat down, taking a pack of Camels from his pocket. His hand trembled as he lit one. "I surely do appreciate you coming down here to see me, Mistuh Tomkins. I'm skeered." He rubbed the graying stubble on his chin and narrowed his eyes against the smoke. "Beggin' yore pardon, suh, but are you the public defender?"

"Kind of, Willy. Call me Mike. I'm a private attorney, but on occasion the public defender's office asks me to represent people. So I'm kind of both—but you're not going to have to pay me anything. That's been taken care of."

"Well, then"—with a gesture of finality, he carefully tamped the cigarette out in the metal ashtray, touched the end to make sure it was cool, and tucked it back into the pack—"I want a real lawyer."

I sighed. This was the typical reaction of most criminals, I knew—or at least it had been. People thought that public defenders were "sort of" attorneys. The old American idea that you get what you pay for is still pervasive. Since public defenders are free, goes the reasoning, there must be a catch.

That may have been true at one time, when courts would appoint an attorney who was just standing around the courtroom when somebody was arraigned. Sometimes a lawyer would be asked to represent an individual, and the individual would end up with an attorney who knew nothing about criminal law—who might, in fact, be a securities specialist.

The appointed lawyer could not say no, and would be paid very little. He'd be unhappy, and the defendant wouldn't be happy, either, since his freedom then depended on a nonspecialist in the criminal area who would defend him only because he had to.

This is no longer the case. In metropolitan areas, a public-defender system is used. The public defenders are the opposite of prosecuting attorneys. Salaried criminal specialists, they are highly motivated and almost by definition politically liberal. They wouldn't know a statutory warranty deed, for instance, if it came into their office and bit them in the ass. Nor should they. As in every other profession, specialization is the new name of the game.

"I am a real lawyer, Willy."

He peered suspiciously at me, still fingering his chin. Then he nodded. "Okay."

"Now," I said, uncapping my pen and pulling the legal pad toward me, "if I'm going to defend you, I need to know what happened in as much detail as you can remember, all right? What time was it when you got into trouble?"

"Whut do you mean?" He leaned forward, reaching again

for the Camels. His body odor was as thick as his Alabama drawl.

I moved back in my chair. "Do you know what you're charged with?"

"Kind of." He stared at a point above my left shoulder. "Doing it to a little girl."

"When?"

"Tuesday."

"What time Tuesday?"

"Late . . ."

Most people do not know how to tell a story. This is true in both the civil and criminal fields of law. They immediately leap into the high points of a story, without identifying people, places, or reasons. These are the most important things that an attorney needs to know. In a criminal case, what happened hours before the crime—physical and psychological motivation—may be the most important thing.

"Okay, Willy," I suggested, "start at twelve o'clock Tuesday afternoon."

It seems that Tuesday had been a rather uneventful day for Willy Buford, at least until Mrs. Oakes asked him to baby-sit. Mrs. Oakes, a woman of about thirty-five who lived in the same apartment complex as Willy and his wife, had apparently had a hot date. In a pinch for a baby-sitter, she asked Mr. Buford, a passing acquaintance, if he could help her out.

Willy allowed as to how he'd be proud to oblige, and leaving his bride of four months at home, had shown up promptly at eight. Mrs. Oakes promised to be home by midnight, and admonished four-year-old Teresa to be a good girl and to mind Mr. Buford.

Teresa showed Willy her dolls and her toys, and was obedient when he put her to bed at around eleven. She was asleep by eleven-fifteen.

There was no TV in the apartment. Willy got bored. He went downstairs to his sixty-seven Rambler with headrests and removed a bottle of white port wine he'd stashed behind the back seat. Sitting in the front seat, he polished off the whole thing, and returned (a trifle unsteadily, I assumed) to the apartment.

Sometime later—he wasn't sure just when—he heard the little girl pad to the bathroom. He stuck his head in to make sure everything was okay. After she was done she left her panties on the bathroom floor.

"Willy, this is real important. Did she leave the panties there, or did *you* take them off and leave them there?"

"I can't rightly remember, Mr. Tomkins. It's all so fuzzy."

"Try, Willy."

He screwed up his face in concentration. "I think she did."

"Why do you think so?"

He didn't answer.

"Willy, are you saying that because I want to hear it or are you saying that because it's true?"

"I just can't rightly remember, Mr. Tomkins." He shook his head sorrowfully. "It's that white port wine. I shoulda never drank it."

"How blitzed were you?"

"Parn?"

"How drunk were you?"

He hitched his chair closer. "Well, look," he said confidentially, "I got a regular capacity for likker, except when I drink white port wine. I shoulda never drank it."

"That's not the point, Willy. How drunk were you?"

"I tell you, Mr. Tomkins, that white port wine—that stuff makes me do crazy things."

"Are you saying that you have an alcohol problem," I asked hopefully, "and didn't know what you were doing?"

"No, suh." Positively. "I kinda knew what I was doing, but I didn't want to do it. That white port wine . . ."

"So you don't have an alcohol problem."

"No, I purely do not."

Most serious crimes involve an element of intent. The

prosecution must prove that the individual intended to do a physical act and that the individual would know the consequences of that physical act. The legal terminology involved here is *mens rea*, literally, guilty mind.

If a person becomes drunk by his own hand, the fact that he is intoxicated is not a defense to an act such as murder or robbery. If a person is so drunk that he doesn't even remember that he robbed or murdered, that in itself is no defense. But the fact that he was so intoxicated that he could not form the volitional intent to commit the crime might be.

On the other hand, it may be a complete defense if a teetotaler went to a party and became intoxicated by drinking what he believed to be nonalcoholic punch, and then, not recognizing the symptoms of drunkenness, set fire to his wife.

"So what happened after she went to the bathroom, Willy?"

"Well, I think I led her back to the bedroom—this is all kind of fuzzy—and I tucked her into bed. Then I . . . I think I got on top of her and she started to cry a little bit . . ."

This is a typical response: Most defendants are reluctant to talk in detail about those events which show them in an evil or unflattering light, even though they're probably in jail precisely because of those events. In a sex crime such as this, the reluctance is more intense.

"Okay, Willy, did you penetrate her?"

He blinked. "Whut do you mean?"

"Did you get inside her? With your penis?"

"I don't think so. I don't ever . . ."

I took this information with relief. This was my first child molester, after all, and I had the same sort of feelings that anybody else would have about him. I hung onto the fact that he hadn't penetrated her. I hoped it was true as a justification that, if the child was not physically penetrated, possibly there would be less physical or psychological harm done. I hoped this would be confirmed by the medical report.

"Willy, you know I will do everything I can to get you off on this thing, but our first order of business is getting you out of jail and back on your job so you can support your wife."

"I rightly appreciate that, Mr. Tomkins. The wife's expectin' . . ." He ducked his head bashfully, as if expecting congratulations.

He just blew my impotence theory, I thought glumly. "You know, Willy, this is a serious crime, one that calls for up to twenty years in the slammer. I need to know if you've ever had any convictions for anything—especially sex-related offenses."

"No, I haven't."

"I have to know the truth, Willy. It's going to come out anyway. It'll just save me time if you're honest. I don't mean just convictions, I mean trouble of any kind."

He lit another Camel, his faded blue eyes focusing above my shoulder again. "Well, once in California, about six years ago, they asked about a little thing. But they found out it wasn't me."

"Were you arrested?"

"I don't think so."

"Did you have to go to court?

"No. I told you," he whined, "it wasn't me."

"Okay. That's going to be helpful. Anything else?"

"No."

I knew that he was lying. Or trying hard not to remember. My instincts screamed that he was hiding something from me. Was this information going to be serious, I wondered— or deadly?

I made a note to check his past record carefully when I received the discovery material from the prosecuting attorney. I tucked my pad and book back in the briefcase. "Okay, Willy. Here's my card. If you need to get in touch with me, don't call the public defender. I'm not a public defender, remember. Call the number on the card, talk to my secretary, Jean. And I'll see you at the bail hearing."

"Much obliged, Mr. Tomkins." He stuck his small sticky hand through the bars and shuffled away—a sad middle-aged man in too-large jail clothes.

"I don't even want to hear about it," said Lamb, clicking shut his briefcase and straightening his tie. "I'm gone for the day, Jean," he said leaving.

Jean watched him leave, a thoughtful expression on her face. "Hmm. Well, anyway, Michael, I do want to hear about it. Are you going to take the case?"

"I never really decided to—but I guess I will." I retrieved a Coke from the tiny refrigerator in our supply room and returned to the couch by Jean's desk. "He's everything I thought he would be—a pathetic little scumbag of a guy."

"No question but that he did it, I suppose."

"No question at all." I sighed. "He says the white port wine made him do it. The little girl is only four."

"Brother."

"Yeah. I guess I can just try to get him the best deal I can."

"So you are going to take the case." Jean smiled. "I thought you would, Michael. Somebody has to—and it's not your job, remember, to justify or excuse what he's done, or even to deny that he did it. I do think, though, that you might want to look into that sexual offender program at Western State. Anybody who'd do something like that must be sick and need help much more than imprisonment."

"Yeah. He wouldn't last very long in prison anyway."

"Hi," Judith stepped into the door of my place carrying a large bag of groceries. We'd taken to eating dinner most nights at her place or mine. Prosser bounded to greet her with his usual joy, probably hoping he'd find someone to talk to with more to say than I'd had that afternoon. "I have some fantastic news."

She set the groceries on the kitchen cabinet. "Look what I got today." She dug in her purse and produced a thick envelope and presented it to me with a flourish.

It was postmarked Atlanta, Georgia, and bore the imprint of the Yerkes Regional Primate Research Center. "They want me to send my resume and three letters of recommendation." She bustled around, unpacking food. "Isn't that wonderful? Maybe I have a chance at it yet."

"That's just great, Judith." I tried, I really tried to put some joy into my voice for her sake. I didn't consider that good news in the slightest, since if she was accepted, she would leave just after the first of the year. I didn't want her to go. I understood how important her career was to her—but Atlanta was too far away, and I just didn't want her to go.

"You don't sound pleased in the least." She looked at me, hands on hips. "We won't talk about Atlanta right now, because I think you were feeling down when I got here, right? Did something happen at work today?"

As we chopped and sautéed, preparing dinner, I told her about Willy.

"I can understand why you're feeling down. It must have been horrible to sit there listening to him and know that he didn't have the faintest idea that what he'd done could have hurt that little girl seriously." She reached over to take an olive from the salad I was assembling.

I slapped her hand away. "No nibbles. Actually, I wasn't thinking that at all. I just went to work, taking notes and asking him about the things I had to ask about. I didn't really start thinking about him until later."

"You know," she said thoughtfully, when we were sitting at the table, "since he doesn't really deny that he did it, and since you can't go bombing into court yelling about 'tragic miscarriage of justice' and all that, what you could do—and this would be a very positive way of handling this case, Mike—would be to make it possible for Willy to get the treatment he needs."

"Jean said the same thing. There's a sexual offender program at Western State I'm going to check into. But it's probably pretty crowded, and the standards for acceptance might be so high that Willy can't meet them."

"So he'll probably end up in prison, right?"

"I think so. I'm positive he has a prior record of this kind of thing, and they aren't going to let him walk around loose any more."

"Can't you do something? Prison won't do him any good."

"It's too early to tell yet. Maybe I can figure out something when I have more information."

"What did Lamb say?"

"He didn't even want to hear about it. It's bad enough that he had to deal with people all the time—God forbid any of them should be criminals."

"Do I detect a note of bitterness?"

"I'm just tired. You know what it costs to keep a guy like Willy in prison, Judith? It cost sixteen thousand dollars a year. That's no special programs or anything like that—just prison. Or maybe its twenty thousand dollars a year. I think it varies from state to state. That's just to warehouse the Willies in this country. Then they get out some day, worse than when they went in. Absolutely no one benefits from a system like that."

"I know," Judith said, taking her plate to the kitchen. "There's got to be a better way than that."

"I've devised one," I said, following with my plate. We went to the living room, turned on the news. "I pick a council of ten people. Poor, rich, all colors and creeds and both genders. They in turn pick a council of one hundred—an even larger cross section—who then pick a council of a thousand. By this time, these thousand people should represent all walks of life, all political persuasions, employed, unemployed. As a safety mechanism, this jury will be slightly overbalanced in favor of ACLU types. It will receive a detailed dossier on the accused, prepared by social workers, doctors, family members, friends, enemies, police—anybody who might have knowledge of the life and times of the accused.

"When the jury has had a chance to become thoroughly acquainted, as much as possible, with the accused, the accused is brought out to answer questions from members of the jury. After this dialogue, the jury will vote by pushing one of two buttons. Red or green. If nine hundred red lights go on, a trapdoor opens, the chair upends and the accused drops into the alligator pit, where nature takes it course. No appeals, no stalling techniques, no reassessments. It's over. Cleanly and right now.

"There are limits to who may appear in front of the jury. No one under twenty-eight years old can appear. Most people just don't know enough about life before then to have it make sense. People change—get religion or get smarter. So twenty-eight is a fair age. And the only people who can appear before the jury must have *hurt* somebody."

Judith tried to interrupt at this point, but I didn't stop talking. It felt good to say it all, finally.

"It seems there are certain people who are social psychopaths, killers, genetic misfits. Maybe it's not their fault in some broad social or moralistic view, but the fact remains we are confronted with more and more people and fewer and fewer resources. These people are takers—they don't give anything back."

"But mistakes could be made, and they'd be irrevocable ones," said Judith quietly.

"Mistakes are made now. Maybe Caryl Chessman didn't do it. The Rosenbergs, on the other hand, wouldn't even go before the jury. Let me finish. The council of ten sits for one nomination session—and can only appoint one council of ten, and so on. They sit for twelve months. The power is then so diluted that no one person—ever—decides anything that could be detrimental to the society as a whole."

"Are you through?"

"Yep." I felt much better. "And I didn't just say it as a result of Willy. I've been mulling this idea around in my head for years."

"I know this is going to surprise you," said Judith, "but I think it's a pretty good idea." She moved to turn on the television. "I don't feel like doing a thing tonight except watching some silly situation comedy."

"Me, too. I'm about all talked out, for a change. Maybe there's even a good movie on." I was exhausted.

"Yeah. Maybe they're rerunning *Lolita*," said Judith.

The bail hearing was days later. Over the eye-rolling protests of the prosecutor, I arranged to have Willy released on bail. After all, as I pointed out, he had no record of any sort of offense such as this—that we knew of at that time, anyway.

Willie's wife was present, and she accosted me after the hearing to pump my hand and heap glad cries of thanks on my head. Fat, wearing a faded dress and bedroom slippers, she looked like a woman who would marry Willy. Her face and neck were covered with hair-sprouting moles. "I'm right proud to meet you, Mr. Tomkins. And thank you. I aim to go right now and fix the bail and get him out. We're expectin' a young one in the winter, and I don't know what I'd do if I didn't have Willy by my side." She patted her belly, beaming.

"Glad to be of help, Mrs. Buford." But actually, I felt a headache coming on, and also felt that I richly deserved the sneer from the prosecutor as he passed us in the hall.

The phone rang around eleven. "Tomkins."

"Mr. Tomkins?"

"Yeah."

"This is Sergeant Meara of the city police. We have a problem here. I think you should come down. Is Willy Buford your client?"

Oh, God. "Yes, he is."

"Well, please get down here as soon as possible."

"Can you tell me what the—where is Willy?"

"At his home. We're all here."

"Hey, can you give me an idea of what's going on?"

"Just get here." He hung up.

Willy lived in a run-down apartment complex on the edge

of town. I broke all land records in getting there. I had a headache, and I was hungry, and I couldn't imagine what was going on at Willy's place.

Whatever it was, it must be mighty interesting, I thought, as I neared the apartment parking lot. Red police lights revolved slowly, lighting the faces of the crowd (which looked to number about two hundred people, but probably didn't). I parked behind the police cruiser and pushed my way through the people. Willy sat huddled in one of the patrol cars, gnawing on a knuckle.

I thumped on the window. "Willy—"

One of the officers approached and pushed me away from the car. "Who the hell do you think you are?" he asked, eyeing my sweat shirt and jogging pants.

"I'm Mike Tomkins, officer, Mr. Buford's attorney. What's going on?" The crackle and static of the police radios intermittently drowned out the shouts of the crowd.

The officer was young and scared, but tried to cover it up. He straightened with the sound of creaking leather. "We received a call about an hour ago. People were battering his door," he indicated Willy with his chin. "And we were trying to get him out of here when he asked us to call you." He removed his hat, ran a hand through his hair. "We found a rope."

Oh, God. By now people in the crowd had noticed me talking to the officer and I could hear distinct shouts and murmurs. "Who is that guy? Who is he?"

"You've got to get him out of here," said the officer. I noticed his name tag. Meara.

"You're the guy who called me. Why do I have to get him out of here? Where am I going to take him?"

"He said you'd know." Again he indicated Willy with his chin. "We've called for assistance, but we figure if you get him out of here the crowd will go on home. Is it true he molested a little girl? The neighbors are pretty upset."

"Oh, Jesus." I'd done my job too well. Willy might have

been better off in jail, at least this night. "I don't have the faintest idea where to take him."

"You got him out. Why don't you take him to your place?" He smirked. "He can't stay here." He rocked back on his heels, proud as if he'd spoken the wisdom of a sage.

A rock sailed through the air, striking the patrol car. "Let's go," said Meara, opening the door and pushing me in beside Willy.

"Oh, Mr. Tomkins, I'm right glad to see you," he blubbered, flinging himself across my lap. "I don't know where to turn." I noticed that he hadn't bathed since leaving jail, and his body odor was worse in the enclosed car.

"Just relax, Willy." I tried to breathe through my mouth. "Is there anywhere you can spend the night?"

"My wife's people. She—my wife—don't want them to know nothin' about this, though. I mean the trouble and all. So I thought if you could drive me over there, it's gonna look a sight better than coming up in a po-lice car."

"Okay. I'll take you there." I shoved him firmly to the other side of the car and tapped on the glass separating us from the officers in the front.

It was well into the early morning by the time I had returned with Officer Meara to pick up my car, fetched Willy (as he put it) to his in-laws, declined his father-in-law's offer of a "little snort" and gotten home to bed.

I'd had second thoughts about taking the case in the first place, but now there was no ambivalence. I wished I'd never met Willy Buford.

The following day I received the discovery material from the prosecutor. As much as I wished I'd never learned of Willy's existence, he was my problem now. And a problem he was indeed.

Discovery material is that material which the prosecuting attorney is obligated to give to the defense attorney, on the theory that both sides have a right to know, prior to trial, with what they are dealing. No longer is a trial a matter of showmanship, in which Perry Mason can confound a jury by sashaying through the double doors with a surprise witness, to the accompaniment of gasps from the spectators and the judge furiously pounding his gavel and demanding order, order in the court.

It is felt that the truth can be arrived at much better by allowing two adversaries, equally matched, in what should properly be a trial of fact, rather than a theatrical battle of tactics.

So when I read the material the prosecution had sent on Willy, which was everything that the national computer had coughed up, I had ample reason to be apprehensive.

There was the little matter in Alabama: Willy had been arrested for child molestation there, and had been sentenced to thirty days of psychiatric observation and a one year suspended sentence on the condition that he remove himself with all possible speed from that state.

There was the ten-year-old girl in the same apartment building where Willy and the Missus lived now who had complained that Willy had "touched her all over."

It didn't look good.

"Look, Willy," I told him in my office, "you don't have one thing going for you at this time. If you plead guilty, I think I can get you into a hospital where you can get help—"

He stuck out his lip. "I didn't do nothin' wrong."

This was a constant. He didn't seem to understand that if he didn't cooperate with me, I wouldn't be able to get him admitted to a hospital, and he'd be spending the next twenty years in prison.

I tried again. "The judge is allowed quite a bit of discretion in cases like this, Willy. We can get you into a hospital—a nice one, where your wife can come and visit you. And then you can get out when you're better. That could be as soon as a year." The connecting door to Lamb's office slammed shut.

"It was the white port wine, Mr. Tomkins. If we tell the judge that I won't drink no white port wine . . ."

This was not going to be easy, I thought gloomily. I had nothing. Absolutely nothing. If we went to trial, about the only thing I could do would be to put the little girl on the stand. I could see myself now: "Isn't it true, Teresa, that you deliberately wore your most seductive Dr. Dentons? And isn't it further true that you enticed Mr. Buford into the bathroom . . ."

I tried another tack. "I know it was the white port wine, Willy. And you know it. But maybe for a while we could sort of pretend that you have a problem, and that way you could go to the hospital for a while. You'd be out real soon so you could be with your wife."

He chewed nervously on a fingernail. "She don't want me to go away. She's expectin', you know."

"I think that's wonderful," I said heartily. "And now you have responsibilities, Willy. The sooner you're out of the hospital, the sooner you can take care of your little family."

He squinted at me. "You sure I can be out in a year?"

"Well . . . as soon as you're better. It could be that soon."

"Okay."

I hustled him out of the office before he could change his mind, and called the prosecutor.

If we pled guilty, he said, he'd go along with me in recommending hospitalization. His trial schedule was terrible, and he'd be glad to recommend a ninety-day observation period.

The sex-offenders unit of the state mental hospital is a select operation. Only the "good" sex offenders—those with a definite chance of rehabilitation—are accepted. I was pleased that in spite of overcrowding and understaffing, Willy would have his period of observation. In order to get into the program, he had to be under the jurisdiction of the court. I was glad that everything was working out so well.

A few weeks later I received a call from Dr. Robert Schwartz, the head of the program. "Your star pupil has got to go, Mike," he said. "I'm sorry. Willy Buford just isn't working out here."

"Oh, come on—"

"He continues to insist that he doesn't have a problem, he refuses to take responsibility for his actions, he remains uncommunicative during sessions, he is disruptive to the others. It just isn't working."

"But you've only had him there"—I flipped frantically back through my calendar—"eighty-five days. You agreed to observe him for ninety."

Schwartz sighed. "Look. I have too many people waiting to get into this group. I have too few trained people to help them, and I can't take up space and time for Willy Buford."

"You mean he still says he didn't do it?"

"Oh, no. He admits he did it all right. But it isn't his fault, you see." Dr. Schwartz's voice was heavy with irony. "It was that white port wine."

"Can't you give him some more time, doc? His family situation is changing—his wife's going to have a baby . . ."

"I've met Mrs. Buford," Schwartz said drily. "She says he just gets 'likkered up sometimes' and goes out of his head."

"That woman could be a tower of strength for Willy," I said stoutly. "Oh, look, I know all that's bullshit. But you may have already helped him more than you know. How do you know he's not just a month or so away from taking a good look at himself?"

Silence. I could hear Schwartz breathing. "Okay," he said. "Forty more days. But that's *it*, Tomkins. You understand?"

I called Willy. "What the hell are you *doing* up there?" I shrieked. "You have a chance to stay in a nice place, to get out in a reasonable amount of time and make something of your life. What the hell are you *doing*?"

"They made me angry," he said. "The things they say."

"You'd better start listening to some of the things they say. They're probably for your own good. And think of your wife."

I did manage to elicit a promise from Willy—a promise of

sorts that he would try to behave. "I'll try to do right," he told me.

It wasn't good enough, though, because less than a month later, Schwartz called me again.

"I can't help Willy. This program isn't geared to that kind of therapy. And there's somebody out there right now who could profit from what we do. Willy's just taking up space. I'm really sorry, Mike."

"I know you did your best, doc. Same old thing?"

"Yeah." He sounded tired. "It'll all be in my report to the court."

The day that Willy was sentenced to prison, the judge asked him why he felt that the sex offender program didn't help him.

"They made me angry," was all that Willy would say before they took him away.

His wife sat in the rear of the courtroom, clutching a cracked leather pocketbook, tears running in crooked silvery streaks down her round face. She watched me as I left. As I passed her, she said, "Mr. Tomkins, Willy never meant no harm. He drinks a little too much sometimes, but he's a good man."

There was nothing more I could do, so I touched her shoulder. "Yes, he is," I said, feeling sorrow for this sad mole-sprouting woman and her pathetic little husband.

We just have no place for people like Willy. The sex offender program is the only one of its kind in the state, and it is forced to be as selective as it is. We don't vote enough tax dollars to provide the personnel or facilities to care for all the Willies. That kind of economy makes sense to the middle class, upon whose shoulders the burden rests.

I imagined a shirt-sleeved politician at the Fourth of July picnic, stumping for improved facilities for child molesters and perverts. Then I imagined this same politician climbing down from the platform and reaching for a baby to kiss.

Even I wouldn't vote for him.

Chapter 8

"Did Mr. and Mrs. Garrison say why they were coming in today?" I asked Jean.

"Sounded pretty routine. They want help with the adoption of their foster daughter, and then a new will."

"Who are Mr. and Mrs. Garrison—ax murderers? Or a husband-and-wife arson team?" Lamb leaned in my doorway, smiling.

He'd been doing reasonably well, taking up the slack with the subrogation cases from Cascade Insurance and taking a few cases of his own here and there. He'd just gotten a big divorce case, referred from another attorney, that was going to require hours of complicated tax research. For him, that sort of activity equaled bliss.

"They're probably just normal people, Lamb. Most of my clients are."

"Uh-huh. Compared to you, maybe they're normal. I'm off to the law library." He left, neglecting to say good-bye to Jean.

"Am I imagining things, or are you and Lamb both a little tense this week?"

"Very astute, Michael." Jean shook her head. "It's no big thing."

"Well, tell me."

"It's just that yesterday afternoon he handed me a final draft of a contract he'd drawn up. He wanted it typed 'right away.' That was no problem. But as soon as I started to do it 111 up, I noticed that the names had been transposed. I knew they were, since he's had that file around for months now."

"So he made a mistake."

"That wasn't the problem. When I went in and said, 'I think you might want to check this,' he didn't even raise his eyes. He just said, 'I only expect you to type, Jean, not to think. Just do as you're told, for once.' So I did. I just typed it, knowing it was wrong."

I started to smile. "And you mean to tell me he had to take the contract with the errors in it to a meeting with his client?"

"No, he didn't do that," Jean was trying not to laugh. "I think he came in very early and typed it over himself. The margins on my typewriter had been reset when I got here."

Just then the door opened and Sharon and Bill Garrison came in with their daughter Lisa, a crowing toddler with cinnamon-colored skin and two adoring parents.

"For three years she's been our daughter, and we want to make it official," said Sharon, restraining Lisa from climbing up the coatrack. "We'd like to make her ours for keeps."

The Garrisons were a handsome couple. Bill was a lineman for the phone company, and had the ruddy complexion of the outdoorsman. Sharon was petite, her dark hair carefully styled—cute rather than beautiful, with a surprisingly stubborn chin. I liked them both.

Bill and Sharon could not have children of their own, and took in Lisa as a foster child to learn what parenting is all about, since they'd been discussing adoption.

"We'd like you to handle the adoption, Mike," said Bill.

"Shouldn't be any problem," I said. "There'll be a hearing—just a formality—to determine the best interests of the child. I'll set a date for juvenile court, and when I do, you'll hear from me. Seems like this will be pretty routine."

The state pays families to care for children who have been abused or abandoned. In order to be free to do this, the state moves for a dependency hearing. The state is represented by a prosecuting attorney, who is a civil attorney. The state then petitions the court to declare that the child be a permanent ward of the court and thus available for adoption by an agency or individuals such as foster parents.

All parties who may have an interest in the child are given the opportunity to appear and answer through counsel. In this case, according to the information I received from the Garrisons, the mother had taken off and abandoned the child shortly after her birth. The father was an American Indian in jail for manslaughter. For reasons known only to himself, he had retained Indian Legal Services to stop the state from allowing the Garrisons to adopt Lisa. Apparently he wished to have the child sent to his relatives in Oklahoma—the relatives who were Lisa's Indian relatives.

When notice of this was received, the court appointed a guardian ad litem (guardian for the legal procedure) to represent the child. Sometimes referred to as "next friend," the guardian ad litem is appointed in all cases in which the welfare of a child is or could be at issue, such as divorce cases, delinquency procedures, or adoption. No longer can a child be caught between two litigants like a minnow between battling whales.

I notified Sharon and Bill of the hearing date, entered it on my calendar, and didn't give it another thought.

Present at the first hearing were myself, the attorney for the father, the attorney for the mother (who, because he'd had no contact with his client, just sat there and could contribute nothing), the state attorney representing the Department of Social and Health Services, the guardian ad litem for Lisa, and an attorney from Indian Legal Services, representing the father's interests. These hearings are routine, the court being interested to know if anybody objects to the child's being permanently taken from his birth parents.

The attorney for the state explained that the mother was an alcoholic, sometime prostitute with health problems, and that she had skipped town. No one knew how to contact her. The last time the social service people had any contact with her was seven months ago. Two social workers testified to these facts.

Next, I put Bill and then Sharon on the stand. They testified that as foster parents they wanted to be able to adopt Lisa. The baby was not aware of her birth parents; she viewed the Garrisons as her parents.

The guardian ad litem then made an oral report to the court on behalf of his client, Lisa, agreeing with the state's petition to relinquish custody of the child to the state.

All was going as I'd expected it to. I smiled at Sharon Garrison, who was watching the proceedings with great interest.

Then the attorney for the incarcerated father objected to the granting of the state's petition on grounds of ethnic and cultural deprivation. "We will show, your Honor," he said, "that Native American children are being adopted into white homes. The practice is a cancer eating at the lifeblood of a race already diminished by war and poverty. We are a minority on the brink of extinction, your Honor, and we object to the continued drain of our children from our way of life."

No one knew what the hell this attorney was saying. Nor what the legal standing of his arguments was in relation to this particular hearing. It was very quiet.

The judge looked perplexed, not expecting that this routine paper-pushing matter would have been contested in any real sense. After a short series of questions, he determined that a fact-finding hearing should be held to further explore Mr. Whitepaw's arguments based on his social theories of Native American rights.

I objected. "Your Honor, this matter was set for today. All parties were aware that this matter was going to be heard today. I personally had no notice that this issue as a basis for rejection of the DSHS petition would be put forth. Counsel for the father should have had the courtesy to inform the interested parties of his objection. Further, your Honor, I see no reason, and I have heard of no legal basis, why this matter should not be decided at this time. Testimony as to the best

welfare of the child has been heard, with no factual opposi-
tion presented except the speculative, unsubstantiated, and
irrelevant remarks of counsel. Court rules require that the
matter, in the event that it is contested, be set over to an
appropriate time. To my knowledge, this was not done."

"All of this is true, Mr. Tomkins," said the judge. "And I
must say, Mr. Whitepaw, your position and timing are most
distressing. This court is not impressed with your arguments."

Whitepaw spoke quiet forcefully. "Your Honor, I
apologize if my position is not timely, but my client communicated his position to me, quite adamantly, on Tuesday
morning. I didn't have time to inform the court. However,
this issue must be fully examined and I must insist that this
matter be reset."

"I am inclined to deny your motion, Mr. Whitepaw, but if
appealed, my decision would probably be overturned. I'll set
this matter for Tuesday next at nine-thirty in this courtroom." We all rose as he left the room.

Bill and Sharon were at my side in seconds. "What the hell
happened?" asked Bill. "You said this was going to be
routine. How can this father guy, who's sitting in the slammer, have any rights, let alone hold up this procedure?"

"To be honest, Bill, I'm surprised as well. But it looks like
we're going to have to confront issues that we weren't prepared to confront. So it looks like the extra two weeks are
going to do me a world of good. I'll need the time to prepare."

Sharon twisted her rings. "Is this still going to cost what
you quoted—three hundred dollars? I don't know if we can
afford—" She stopped talking when Bill touched her arm.

"Don't worry about the money," I told them, holding the
courtroom doors open. "The important thing is getting your
child adopted. Now, I know you're freaked out—you weren't
expecting this. I wasn't either."

"What happens now, Mike?" Bill put his arm around Sharon.

"I research all cases I can find on similar situations. But the main legal point, the main concern of the court and what the judge's decision will have to be based on, is the welfare of the child, what's in Lisa's best interest. And that means you and Sharon."

During the next weeks, I prepared a trial brief for the judge so he would be acquainted with current law on this subject.

"You're certainly putting in a lot of time on this one, Mike," Judith said, after the third exciting night at my place watching me pore over books. "I can understand Whitepaw's point, I guess. But it would seem to me that he should direct his energy to promoting adoption among his own people instead of tackling the issue through the Garrisons."

"Well," I told her, "the research I'm doing makes me feel better, anyway. The judge is going to listen to all the evidence, even that from Whitepaw, and then decide that the best thing for Lisa is Sharon and Bill. I have no doubt of that."

The next day, though, I got dumped on. Whitepaw called, advising me that he was sending over some documents which he would be introducing at time of trial. These documents, he assured me, would show that the issue in general was not really this Indian child, but non-Indians adopting the babies of a nation struggling to hold onto its cultural identity. "All of a sudden," he said, "a lot of middle class 'white kids' have dark skin and eyes. It's simple, really, Mike," he continued. "Lisa is a Native American. She should be brought up as a Native American, and not as a Wasp. I've advised the father against relinquishing. We'll talk when you've read the material and have had a chance to understand more about our point of view."

Later that afternoon the messenger arrived, bent almost double under the weight of the material from Whitepaw. It filled a cardboard carton. Books, pamphlets, briefs—more stuff than I could read in a month, even if I'd graduated from Evelyn Wood.

I made a brave beginning, though. The basic problem was this: Indian children when they were abandoned, were turned over to the child-care division of the Department of Social and Health Services. The guidelines for placing such children were based on middle-class white values. A Native American family wanting a foster child (and there were admittedly not too many such families due to the continuing economic problems of such families) could not qualify. No indoor plumbing, for instance, or no employed male head of family.

Since social workers are deathly afraid of giving a foster child to a family who wants or needs the monthly check for the child's care, Indian families rarely received Indian children. The children are placed in middle-class white homes. In many cases, like Lisa's, love grows naturally, the next step adoption. Another "lost" Indian.

This case was turning into a cause célèbre—and I did not want a cause célèbre. They cost a lot and are very time-consuming. All this ballyhoo couldn't be of any possible benefit to my clients.

This was a civil action, and in matters such as this, Legal Aid is the poor man's civil attorney. Legal Aid attorneys do not represent those accused of misdemeanors or felonies; they only represent those defined legally as poor in actions such as divorces, loan-company suits, garnishments—all such civil actions in which the poor might need representation.

Legal Aid offices are funded with a combination of federal, state, county, and city money. They tend to be either very slick operations—like a downtown law firm—or hole-in-the-wall "poverty lawyers."

In Seattle, the poor have the advantages of a sophisticated law firm. This means paralegals, secretaries, computerized business machines, investigators, brief banks, and highly skilled attorneys who are salaried and can afford to spend as much time as it might take to get results.

A brief bank is the ultimate in timesaving services. Any time a lawyer writes a memorandum of law or is involved in a case with possible interest to other members of the firm, a copy is filed for future reference. The brief that I knew Whitepaw was writing was going to read like a master's thesis, if the contents of the cardboard box were any indication.

Bill and Sharon were bewildered. "Why is it different," Bill asked, "for Lisa to be an Indian, and to know it the way I know that my grandparents came from Germany, and Sharon's people came from Finland?"

"They want her to have an appreciation of her culture," said Sharon tightly. "We will do that anyway—we've planned on it. We read about Indians. But dammit, Mike! She's a baby—*my* baby. Not Indian or Chinese, just a baby. Isn't that what this great melting-pot stuff we learned in school is supposed to be all about?"

"You're right, you're both right," I said. "And if the welfare of Lisa is the only thing the court will consider, and it is—then you'll win."

As the date of the trial approached, more and more material arrived from Whitepaw. We communicated by phone, each conversation as aimless and as inconclusive as our first. Legal Services obviously was devoting a lot of time to this matter. The guardian ad litem was an overworked suburban attorney. I spoke to him, and he felt that there could be no question of what was best for the child—she should be allowed to stay with her parents. And as far as he was concerned, her parents were Sharon and Bill. He had no idea what Legal Services was doing, or why they were doing it now.

I was as honest as I could be with Sharon and Bill. We arranged for a child psychologist and Lisa's pediatrician to testify. I had the Garrisons prepare to bring Lisa's baby pictures and photo album to the trial. In fact, I told them it would not be such a bad idea to bring Lisa herself.

Sharon would have none of it. "She's a bright little girl, and very sensitive. She'd be sure to understand something of what's going on—not the words, maybe, but something. No, she stays home."

I reviewed my brief. It pointed out that the welfare of the tribe, the welfare of the whole damn Indian nation, for that matter, was irrelevant. This child had been placed by a social welfare agency with the Garrisons only weeks after her birth. The mother had relinquished all rights, and the father had never seen her. The Garrisons were the only parents she had ever had, and to remove Lisa from her home and family could in no way be considered as in her best interests.

I considered my position. Me, with my limited resources, against the almost unlimited resources of a governmental agency. Obviously, I couldn't charge Sharon and Bill the fees to pay for the full-scale legal battle for which Whitepaw was preparing. Legal Services could afford to spend the thousands of dollars necessary—Sharon and Bill could not.

The Senate is concerned now with this very problem. The poor get fine representation for free; the rich can afford the best and highest-priced lawyers. What happens to people like Sharon and Bill? The reason Bill's take-home pay is less than it should be is that he subsidizes these legal services for others while he himself falls through a crack in the system. Much of the discussion about a national legal services plan is concerned with middle-class people.

I did the only thing I felt I could do. I told Bill I'd charge him four hundred dollars no matter how many hours the thing ended up taking.

The trial was going to be concepts against concepts. I wasn't worried about proving my clients were fit, but I didn't want to take any chances. I coached both Bill and Sharon, talked to their pediatrician (who couldn't understand what the hell was going on and offered to help in any way he could). I went to the university and contacted a child psychiatrist who said she would testify also. "I can't afford a witness fee, my clients are really strapped. Could I offer you a free will?"

The trial lasted the better part of two days. Whitepaw presented a stunning collection of facts and statistics illustrating that Indian children were indeed being removed from their tribal culture.

I reminded the court that it was the welfare of one little girl—Lisa—that we were considering here. "This is not the appropriate forum, your honor, to raise the wider sociological issues."

Sharon was dry eyed and composed. She listened attentively throughout the first day. Bill slowly cracked the knuckles of first one big hand and then the other. I was more worried about him than about her.

The judge nodded each time I mentioned "the welfare of the child." Encouraged by this, I mentioned it as often as I had the opportunity. By the time the parade of experts began, I had regained some of my initial optimism.

No surprises there. Our experts spoke of the importance of consistent parental love and nurture, the suitability of the Garrisons as parents, the dire consequences of removing a child from the home and disrupting the primary bonds.

Legal Services' experts spoke of the importance of ethnic identity and the relative unimportance of disrupting a bond while the child was still young enough to have a plasticity of personality.

Although I considered that particular segment of the trial a draw, I remained optimistic at its conclusion. Clearly, since (once again, Mike) the welfare of Lisa was the only issue, and the Garrisons had done splendidly as her foster parents, the matter of their adopting her still appeared to me to be the only logical outcome of the whole thing.

The following day, I put Bill and Sharon on the stand. Our careful preparation paid off. I established that they were loving and devoted parents who cared deeply for the emotional and cultural well-being of their daughter. I felt it was clear to all that they were parents of whom even Dr. Spock would feel proud.

Sharon remained poised and calm, even when Whitepaw cross-examined her. "Mrs. Garrison," he said, "do you know what happened at the north fork of the Duwamish River in 1863?"

"No, I'm afraid not," she answered softly. "But if it is something that Lisa should know, I'd be glad to learn about it."

Bill was the more overtly nervous of the pair. The only time we got in trouble was when he deviated from our carefully planned strategy, and in answer to one of my questions, exploded in an outpouring of frustration and rage against a system he didn't understand.

"I love Lisa," he shouted. "I'll do anything I have to do to make it right with the Indian community and with the court. Goddammit," his voice broke, "I am her father. I'll do what any father would. I'll buy her beaded moccasins and feathers for her hair if it'll help   ." His voice died away, and he sat slumped, shoulders shaking.

Whitepaw was shrewd enough not to object during the outburst, and declined to cross-examine Bill afterward.

Sharon ran sobbing from the courtroom. All the observers coughed and shuffled their feet in unison. It was an uncomfortable moment.

There are three ways an opinion can be handed down from the bench. The judge can make a determination at the close of the case, at which point he will give his reasons for the decision. The only record, then, would be the transcript taken in court. The winning attorney then drafts Findings of Fact and Conclusions of Law, the facts for which he has taken from the judge's words. These are then signed by all parties and the document is then ready to stand as the necessary first step in the process of appealing the decision, should such an appeal be started.

Another way to hand down a decision is for the judge (or rather, his clerk) to write a memorandum of law, citing his decisions and the reasons for them, and the applicable case law upon which his verdict is based. This ensures that no confusion can exist between the judge's decision and the Findings.

If this is to be done, the judge declares that he will "take the case under advisement," meaning that he will study his notes for days or weeks (sometimes even months—there is no time limit for this). It is not uncommon for an attorney to call the judge asking him if the memorandum has been typed yet—a polite way of asking the judge to get off his ass and end the suspense. I am convinced that in certain cases the judge will ask the advice of his wife and kids, and possibly even Al the grocer.

At the end of all the testimony, it was close to three in the afternoon. Court generally adjourns at four. Some judges will continue until they're done; I have, however, known more than one judge who will stop almost in the middle of a sentence when the second hand on the courtroom clock moves onto four o'clock.

I was hoping for a gentlemanly "Thank you, counsel. Fine presentation, but really now—you may have a point about culture and so forth, but the kid stays." It didn't happen.

"Gentlemen," said the judge wearily, "I am faced with a terribly difficult decision. Maybe one of the toughest of my career on the bench. I would like to examine my notes more carefully and read some of the material, including some things from the recent Senate hearings introduced by Mr. Whitepaw.

"I will render my decision next Monday at 9:00 A.M., in order to allow myself the weekend to consider this most troubling question."

We were in trouble, and my clients didn't know it.

"It seems like it went pretty well, didn't it, Mike?" said Bill.

"Yeah," I told him.

The Garrisons decided to stay home from the courthouse on Monday. I promised to call them right away.

The decision was that Lisa's ethnic background was of importance, and therefore, while the Garrisons were considered suitable as foster parents for Lisa, they were not to be considered as adoptive parents of this particular child.

I'd been suspecting it, but when it came, I knew I couldn't

bring myself to call Bill and Sharon and give them the news over the phone. I drove out to their small house in the south end of the city.

Sharon answered the door, Lisa peering from behind. She glanced quickly at my face. "I'll get Bill," her voice was strained. "Come on in."

I waited in the tiny, impeccably neat living room. Lisa climbed across my knees and searched all my pockets with her chubby little hands, laughing at each find. Keys, wallet, pen—all ended up in her lap. She grinned. "Mine," she said.

Bill and Sharon entered the room. "It's bad news, isn't it, Mike?" Bill searched my face, while Sharon opened her arms to Lisa, who ran to her.

"Listen," I said, having to say something. "There's a good chance that she'll be with you for at least another fifteen years. There's no reason for anything to be different now—not really."

Sharon left the room without another word, taking Lisa with her.

"They could take her any time, Mike—and you know it." Bill lowered himself to the couch. "I guess all we can do is pretend the whole thing never happened. We'd have been better off if it never had." He cleared his throat. "It was just a technicality, anyway. She couldn't be any more our little girl."

Incredibly, he was trying to make *me* feel better. "We could appeal the decision," I suggested.

He shook his head. "No. I think we'll just lay low and leave things the way they are. Thanks anyway, Mike. You really worked hard, and we appreciate it."

The judge had said, "In this society, no family can be an island." But as I drove home from the Garrisons, I wondered at the values of a society that tries to do away with islands by forbidding bridges.

Three months later, Lisa was removed from the Garrison's home. I learned that Bill and Sharon got divorced less than a year afterward.

Chapter 9

"Mike, it's good to hear your voice. You sound so grown up ..."

It was Mrs. Kramer calling from California. My parents and the Kramers had been friends since before I was born. I hadn't seen Mrs. Kramer since I'd left for college years before, but there was no mistaking the nostalgic tone of her voice. Next she'd be telling me once again how she used to powder my behind.

"What can I do for you, Mrs. Kramer?"

"I called to tell you that Pammie got married."

"That's wonderful," I said. "Anybody I know?" The Kramer's daughter was five years younger than I.

"He's a Venezuelan boy—just a wonderful fellow. We think very highly of him. There's just one problem, though. He has to apply for his green card, and we thought maybe you could help us out."

"Why me? I'm two states away."

It turned out that in order to apply for a green card from the Immigration Department, Pammie's husband would have to leave the country physically before he could reenter it with the proper credentials. The place he would be reentering from was Vancouver, British Columbia. I, of course, was closer to B.C. than the Kramers' attorney would be. Looking at it that way, I could see that it made sense.

But administrative law, of which immigration law is a sub-

specialty, is a complicated and painstaking business. I had
little experience with it. In fact, I had no experience with it at
all.

"We know this isn't your field, Mike," continued Mrs.
Kramer, "but we have always had a great deal of confidence
in you. And we're so terribly fond of Paulo. So spare no
expense. If you have to consult with an immigration attorney, please don't hesitate. Whatever needs to be done, just do
it. Send us the bill."

The Kramers were loaded. Sam Kramer made money like
other people make mistakes. Throughout my growing up
years he had told me on numerous occasions that making
money was the simplest thing in the world. He was genuinely
puzzled why it appeared to be so difficult for other people to
do it.

This, combined with the edict "spare no expense," convinced me to put my ego and Paulo's future on the line.
"Sure, Mrs. Kramer. Sounds like it'll be interesting."

Dealing with the federal bureaucracy is similar to getting
one's teeth pulled by an army doctor—without Novocain.
You are forced to hurry up and wait so that you can experience exquisite pain.

I knew that in the best of all possible worlds, this case
would take an inordinate amount of time—long-distance
phone calls, dealings with the American Consulate in Canada
via the mails. I wanted to impress upon my clients the tortuous nature of these dealings, which would be almost more
frustrating than they could be expected to bear.

My first task after accepting the case was to find out what
the hell to do. Passing the bar exam qualified me to practice
in Washington, but in no other state. I could also practice in
the federal court systems of all states, with the exception of
the patent courts, which have special requirements of their
own.

Few people realize that there are two distinct legal systems
in the United States—federal and state. There are ten fed-

eral jurisdictions covering the country, in addition to the fifty state systems.

Often, a particular matter will involve both federal and state law. For instance, in the criminal area, the killing of an FBI agent in California: It is against the state law of California to commit murder. Likewise, it is against the Federal Criminal Code to kill a federal officer. It is conceivable that the poor jerk who did it could be tried for the crime in both state and federal court jurisdictions.

In the civil area, if a person was hit by a mail truck that was making an illegal left turn, federal laws would govern. The federal court rather than the state court would have jurisdiction, since a federally owned vehicle was involved.

I knew that I could practice in front of the Immigration Board, which is a federal agency. But what to do in front of it was another matter entirely.

After some time in the legal library, I discovered that I was about to be enveloped in a huge amount of paper pushing.

A lawyer spends a good part of his day pushing paper anyhow—to court to be filed, to his clients to be signed, to the other attorney to be argued over, to his secretary to be typed and/or retyped, and then ultimately back to his own file to be lost forever.

But the documents to be filed with the U.S. Consulate in Vancouver were to be originals, and in triplicate. The amount of information, and the underlying documentation of the triplicate forms was going to require the immediate purchase of a case of Maalox, to be charged to my client and consumed by me.

I realized that Jean and I were going to end up knowing more about Paulo than Pammie did. He was thirty-two years old—old enough to have lived something of a full life, as Jean pointed out—and the consulate was determined to document each ninety-minute segment of it. In triplicate originals.

Everyone in the world, except possibly Americans, realizes

that the United States is in fact the land of milk and honey. People want to get in any way they can. Fraud is a way of life in most South American countries, and one way of getting into the United States is by purchasing counterfeit documentation. The immigration department of the U.S. Consulate, therefore, is a great incentive for these illicit printing presses. Those who work at the consulate may be bureaucrats, but they are not stupid. They realize that there have been tremendous advances in photocopy technology in recent years, and so are adamant that the papers received and processed in their office are originals. Certified originals.

We began the long process of obtaining Paulo's birth certificate, previous marriage and divorce certificate, civil registration, certificate of military service and more, much more.

During the next six months I continually checked with the consulate personnel as to how their companion file was progressing; spoke to Pammie and Paulo, directing them as to which papers I would need next. Jean located a translator, who read and translated military records and employment histories. All went smoothly, if slowly, and I began to relax and congratulate myself on the mastering of a complex procedure.

Then the required police records check uncovered an arrest in early 1970. My clients hadn't told me. They never do.

A quick phone call explained the circumstances. It seems that when Paulo came to the United States he spoke not one word of English. He landed a job paying minimum wage. He was to run a movie projector in an X-rated theater. One week after he started work, the place was raided. The police took Paulo and the ticket taker downtown. Later that day, the theater's attorney came down to jail with appropriate bail and Paulo went back to work.

A month after the arrest he went to court, a procedure about which he understood absolutely nothing. His attorney pled him guilty to a misdemeanor, paid a two-hundred-dollar fine, and Paulo was put on six months' probation. It had all been so casual at the time that Paulo hadn't realized just how important it could become. Until now.

It would have to be explained to the authorities' satisfaction. I had to find out more.

After a trip to California and many phone calls to the theater's attorney (who turned out to be an enormous and uncooperative horse's ass), I discovered that Paulo had been arrested two other times on the same charge—exhibiting obscene material. How this had escaped the notice of the immigration people was unknown to me—but I decided not to volunteer the information.

The next six months were spent completing the file—acquiring sixty original documents, affidavits, pictures, and "certificados"—and keeping the two other arrests a secret.

After some time, I received a letter setting a date for Paulo to meet with the officials in Canada, where the file would be formally processed during the personal interview with the consul general. This meant success—the file was complete.

I was to meet Paulo in Vancouver on the morning of the Big Day, bringing with me the originals which had been reposing for months in my office files, waiting for this occasion. I imagined that there would be no trouble. Canada would determine that the originals in my possession were the originals of the documents they had already approved, and would have another prospective citizen in the land of milk and honey.

I patted my briefcase on the seat of the taxi beside me as the cabbie let me out in front of the consulate. It was 7:45. The weather held little promise of sunshine.

I took the elevator to the third floor, walked a bit nervously down a thickly carpeted corridor, and pushed against the double glass doors. They were locked. A tastefully lettered sign announced: "Open at 8:00 A.M," I waited. At precisely eight the doors were opened by a woman of about Jean's age, uniformed in a blue skirt, blue blouse, police officer's shoes and luminous blue stockings. A small blue triangle hat sat jauntily atop her gray bun. She was clearly the ramrod of this operation.

Paulo joined me as I stood inside the doors. He was tall and handsome, speaking perfect English with a soft accent. I shook his hand, finding it amusing to be just meeting a man about whom I knew so much. His hand was damp. "What do we do now, Mike?" he asked.

"Just take a seat, Paulo," I said, pointing him toward the padded benches against the wall. "I'll see if we can keep our appointment."

An arrangement of velvet ropes and little brass poles arranged people into several lines in the center of the room. They seemed to be waiting to speak to women at what appeared to be tellers' cages. Everybody else seemed to know exactly what to do.

I approached the uniformed woman, who was still patroling the center of the room. I introduced myself. "We have an appointment at eight," I told her.

She looked me over with the disdain that bureaucrats seem to have patented. "Take a seat," she answered through thin lips. "You'll be called."

Well, I'd been right about taking a seat, at least, I thought, as I joined Paulo. I decided to take advantage of the extra time and go through his original documents one more time, in order to be certain that they were in the prescribed order.

I opened my briefcase, pulled out the blue folder . . . and discovered that the documents were not there. They were gone. Absent.

I slammed the briefcase shut. Why does God hate me so? My shirt was soaked in seconds, my brow feverish.

"Is anything wrong?" Paulo asked, eyeing me with concern.

I mopped my forehead, which ran with sweat as if I'd played three sets with Ilie Nastase at high noon. "No, no—nothing wrong. Warm in here, isn't it? Excuse me a minute,

Paulo. I have to call the office and check in. Don't go away—I'll be right back."

The guardian of the front door stared tight-lipped as I asked permission to phone.

"No, I'm sorry. No one may use the phone. It isn't for the use of the public."

"Yes, yes. I understand that. But I'm an attorney from the United States. I'm here with Mr. Ortega. I thought that I could—"

"You thought incorrectly, sir, because you may not use the phone. It is not for the public." She licked her pale lips, relishing the confrontation.

"Is there someone else I could ask?"

"No." A frosty smile began to creep across her face, and she reached up and straightened her little blue hat.

I decided to appeal to her obviously well-developed sense of order. "I seem to have a little problem with this morning's appointment with the consul general and I don't want to inconvenience the staff or interfere with the orderly flow of things . . ."

"You won't."

"Uh, why do you say that?" I sensed that she knew something unpleasant, something that I didn't know. She knew it, and enjoyed that knowledge the way a vulture enjoys the impending death of a rabbit.

"Because," she said softly, triumphantly, "if things are not quite in order, and the case can't be processed on schedule, you won't be seen and must make another appointment."

Well, that wasn't so bad. "You mean for later in the day?" I asked hopefully. Maybe things weren't as bad as they seemed.

"Not for later in the day—for later in the year. These appointments are set up months in advance." She touched her ridiculous hat. "This is a very busy office. If your papers aren't in order by three in the afternoon, the case is set over indefinitely."

"Well," I said casually, restraining a powerful impulse to surround her chicken-skinned neck with my hands, "the problem is a minor one, and can be taken care of by phone. Can you direct me to the nearest one?"

"Certainly. Down to the first floor lobby, out the door, across the alley into the basement of the neighboring building. Now, if you'll excuse me, I have work to do." Back straight, she turned away.

Excuse you? I'd like to cut you into infinite pieces, you supercilious old bag. I marched into the elevator, glaring balefully at her back. I was in serious trouble, if what the old bitch said was correct.

My watch said eight-thirty. I had to call the office, hope Jean was there, have her get on a plane, and fly up to Vancouver. I'd meet her in a cab, grab the documents, fling a twenty at the startled driver and say, "There's another twenty in it for you, buddy, if you make it on time. To the consulate!" Just like in the movies. It sounded possible.

I forced myself to dwell on this possibility and to slow my speeding heart, in order not to think about the other possibilities.

What if Jean were at the office, but the originals weren't! I remembered setting them on my desk with the other papers to go to Canada. I seemed to remember putting them in the briefcase.

The elevator doors opened. I emerged into a lavishly furnished office. As I turned around to get into the elevator to continue the ill-fated quest for a frigging phone, the doors closed behind me. Damn! Wrong floor.

"May I help you?" The lush voice rose from the diaphragm of a gorgeous nineteen-year-old female body. She sat behind a curved wooden desk that rose to my waist from the acres of plush carpeting. My eyes focused on the receptionist of all receptionists. Big blue eyes, cascading blond hair. A bank of telephone buttons glowed and blinked next to her rose-tipped fingers. Telephone light—I'm in heaven. Maybe.

Time was of the essence, so to speak. I couldn't afford to travel four floors down to the lobby, across the alley and further along the strange itinerary planned by the Blue Meanie. But if I could convince this lovely creature to take pity on me, I could save time and energy and maybe—just maybe—get lucky.

"Hi. My name is Mike. I'm an attorney from the U.S. I'm here transacting some business in the consul's office downstairs and I'm having a bit of a problem."

"Oh, that's too bad," she cooed.

"And I was wondering if I might borrow a phone for just a minute. I'll reverse the charges."

She worried her bottom lip with perfect white teeth. "I don't see why not. I've only been here two weeks, and I've been reading the rule book a little every night. I'm not up the part about lending phones, but I'm sure it's all right." She smiled.

I was in love. I would do anything for her—but that would have to come later.

"You know," she said, "you could use the office behind me. No one's in there, and you'll have some privacy."

The large wooden letters on the door read "British Petroleum Company." What a marvelous company, I thought, making a mental note to purchase some British petroleum at the earliest opportunity.

The desk was massive and made of walnut—obviously the desk of a ranking executive.

"You don't have the originals?" Jean's scream would have been clearly audible without the phone.

"No, dammit. Go and look on my desk. If they aren't there, start making funeral arrangements. I prefer a simple, tasteful ceremony—just the immediate family, and Paulo, of course . . ." I was speaking into a dead phone, as Jean had put me on hold. My past whirled through my mind—all the events of a life that had been far too short and uneventful.

"Yes, it's here, Michael. How could you have forgotten it?"

"Jean, shut the hell up. Who cares how? Call the airlines and find out how many flights are leaving and book yourself on the first one. I'll call you back in fifteen minutes."

"I don't think I can do that, Michael. I have four people coming in at different times this morning to sign stipulations. I haven't even started the Wildon trial brief, and—"

"The hell you can't. Call the airlines." I slammed the phone down. At least some progress was being made, I thought, as I gnawed my thumbnail. Even if the documents were a country away, at least they weren't lost.

"Listen," I said to the receptionist, "I certainly appreciate your help. Would you mind if I came back throughout the morning if I needed to? I'm afraid I'm going to have to make several calls turning into quite a problem. By the way, what's your name? I should thank a name, not just a pretty face."

"Ronnie Alexander."

"Ronnie," I said earnestly, "God will remember your acts of kindness." I waved jauntily and boarded the elevator, where I frantically pushed the correct button. Paulo came toward me, looking concerned. "Someone came and took my medical originals, the ones I brought up. But they said they need the others immediately. Is everything all right?"

"Don't worry, Paulo, it's okay. Let them process those—don't want to overwork them, right? Then I'll go take care of the rest. Just have a seat and let me do the worrying."

"I'm glad you're here, Mike. This is so . . ." He paused, searching for the right word. ". . . so bewildering."

"That's what I'm here for, Paulo," I said heartily. Oh, my aching ass, I thought, am I in trouble. I sat by Paulo, checked my watch. Nine-fifteen. Three o'clock was much too close. "Well," I said casually, "Better check in with the office."

"Are you sure everything's all right?"

"Absolutely. Sit tight, Paulo, and I'll be right back."

Back in "my" office I called Jean.

"Only two flights today, Michael—"

"That's impossible."

"—twelve-fifteen and four-thirty," she said impassively.

"I hope you got a reservation for twelve-fifteen."

"Of course I did. It arrives at one-thirty."

"Okay. It will be close, but okay."

"What about Customs?"

"Customs? Oh God—"

"And besides, Michael, I really can't get away. Lamb's in his office. I'll let you talk to him. Perhaps he could run up there. His day is pretty light." She put me on hold.

"Did I hear Jean correctly? You forgot the originals?"

"Boy, Lamb, for once I'm glad to hear your voice. Jean has made the arrangements. If you could just get up here I'd be indebted to you for life. If I can't get those originals into this office by this afternoon, I have to get another date for later in the year and all this will have been for nothing."

"Sorry, Mike. I can't help you. There's some research I was planning to get done today for the divorce trial."

"But that trial isn't until months away—"

"—and I'm an attorney, not a messenger boy." He paused. "I'll give you back to Jean."

"Michael, I heard, and I called Sue Arnold. You know, my friend the sculptor. She says she'll deliver the originals. She said it sounds like an adventure and she believes that adventure is at the core of art. So she'll do it—on one condition. You have to do a will for her."

"A will?" I was limp with relief. "I'll give her *children* if that's what she wants. Just get her wrinkled ass up here as quickly as possible."

I looked up, hearing a discreet cough in the doorway. An older gentleman in tweed stood there with a quizzical look on his face. I broke into my warmest, most sincere smile and waved. The quizzical expression on his face slowly disappeared, to be replaced by a hesitant smile as his hand came up in a tentative wave. He disappeared.

"I'll check with you every hour," I told Jean.

I rose and headed toward the door, intending to thank Ronnie once again.

"Excuse me." It was a woman's voice—clear, authoritarian, belonging to an attractive executive secretary type who stood just outside the door, arms crossed over her ample bosom, as if emulating Mussolini's postspeech balcony manner. "What are you doing in this office?"

"I borrowed your phone for just a moment. I really appreciate your generosity—"

"This is a private office." The arms stayed folded, but an index finger began to tap nonetheless.

"Ah, yes. Well, I'm an attorney. I'm doing some work in the consular office on the second floor and—"

Tap tap went the finger. "Why not use the phone in there?" Flawless logic.

"Well, they don't have any that are—uh, serviceable. Trouble with the circuits or something. The repair people are running late . . ." I smiled at her, inviting her to share my amusement at the peccadillos of laborers.

She was not amused. I think she had heard that before. "We have security here, sir. I'm afraid I'll have to ask you to leave."

"Well, I'll be on my way," I said, suiting action to words, passing Ronnie and avoiding her uncomfortable glance.

Back at the consulate, I scanned the waiting room. Paulo was gone. Oh my God, I thought. They probably sent him back to Venezuela. No. They wouldn't do that. But if I don't figure out where he is, I would consider moving to Venezuela myself.

I took a deep breath and opened one of the blank walnut doors that lined the room. A woman sat poring over a pile of documents, softly questioning Paulo in Spanish. Bingo. As I paused, hesitating, the door opened behind me and I turned to recognize my friend from the lobby, the woman with the glowing blue stockings.

"This is a private room," she hissed.

"Exactly. But I think I should be in here in case of a problem. I put the file together, you see, and Paulo doesn't speak English all that well." That was a lie—Paulo spoke better English than most high school graduates in the United States.

She turned her back in disgust. "Go ahead, then."

Paulo looked relieved to see me. The woman behind the desk rose, extending her hand. "I'm Mrs. Schakley. These documents seem to be in order, Mr. Tomkins—except for some discrepancies in Section twenty-one A dash three point four."

"Of course, of course," I said, taking a seat. "I expected that those would have to be clarified." I turned to Paulo. "Why don't you wait for me out in the reception room."

"Go right ahead, Mr. Ortega," said Mrs. Schakley. "There's really no need for you to sit through all this. As soon as I have corrected the discrepancies and checked the originals, I believe that will be all that is necessary." She smiled kindly at both Paulo and myself.

Paulo left gratefully. I was touched by his simple faith in me, however ill-advised it was.

"Do you have the originals, Mr. Tomkins? I need them so that after I check them Mr. Ortega can have his interview with the consul general. But before I can arrange that, I must verify that all the papers are in order."

"Aren't they?"

"Yes. But—"

"Listen, Mrs. Schakley, the originals are at my office," I said casually. "Now, if they're absolutely necessary, I can have them delivered by my law firm's courier." I thought "courier" sounded a lot more impressive than "art student friend of my underpaid secretary." "You see, there has been a bit of a slip up, but it seems to me that if the copies are in order, that they are obviously copied from originals and therefore the originals exist and are in order, too—so, in point of fact we actually have evidence of them. Rather good evidence, too, I might add." I was really flying now. "So, I'm wondering, since we really have all the needed documents, why we couldn't process the material as scheduled and if absolutely need be, which I'm sure it won't, but if it is, I could procure them at a later date—or possibly this afternoon, as I mentioned, by my firm's courier." I stopped talking, exhausted. My tongue was as dry as if I'd run the mile.

Mrs. Schakely looked up from her desk. "What was that? I beg your pardon, Mr. Tomkins, but I didn't hear you. I was looking at Form DS one-nineteen."

I licked my lips and began again. I said it all, too—only at greater length and even less clearly.

"It's all so irregular," murmured the woman when I had finished. "I don't have the authority to clear a request such as this. I'm supposed to have all the originals and the copies as well."

"Who does have the authority to do that sort of thing?"

"Only the consul general."

That figured, I thought, the head guy. "Well, could I have a moment of his time? Before the interview, I mean?"

"I don't know."

"Who would know?"

"He would—the consul general himself."

I thought of the old saying: That's life. What's life? A magazine. How much? A dime. I've only got a nickel. That's life. Ad infinitum. "Sounds circular, doesn't it?"

"Yes, it does." With typical bureaucratic humorlessness. We sat, saying nothing.

I leaned forward. "I don't want to be difficult, but what about—"

She stood, motioning me to be quiet. "I will put a note in the file. I will then set the appointment for eleven thirty—that's ninety minutes from now. What he decides, he decides." She gave a que será shrug of her shoulders and escorted me to the door. "It's all I can do, Mr. Tomkins."

"So it's possible, isn't it, that he'll waive the originals, or let me bring them at a later date, don't you think?" Hope rose in my breast.

"He never has before. But, yes," she said, as she pushed me through the door and back into the waiting room, "it is possible. But not probable." The door closed with a well-mannered click.

"Everything is fine, Paulo," I assured him as he anxiously came toward me.

"Am I going to have to stay over another day, Mike? I can if I have to, you know."

"Paulo, it's just too early to tell. There are one or two problems that I'm trying to work out with the lady in there, and I'm going to try to see if I can get in to talk to the head guy before our interview. If I can see him, I think it will be okay."

"Are you sure?"

"No, of course not." I tried to force some assurance into my voice. "But I'm doing my best."

Paulo gripped my hand. "That's all anyone can do, Mike. I trust you completely."

I smiled in his direction, not meeting his eyes, and touched his shoulder in a reassuring gesture. I wanted to throw up.

I spent the next hour attempting to get the attention of the consul general, a distinguished gentleman who bustled through the waiting room every so often. After I'd seen him striding along in his charcoal-gray three-piece suit more than four times, I decided to take the bull by the horns, in a manner of speaking.

I made my move. "Excuse me, Mr. Nabors. My name is Mike Tomkins. I'm Mr. Ortega's attorney. I don't know if Mrs. Schakley has had an opportunity to speak to you about a little problem that has arisen . . ." From the corner of my eye I could see the blue-uniformed sentinel approaching at four o'clock. I attempted to push Mr. Nabors from her path, but it was no good.

"Sir, Mr. Nabors is on an extremely tight schedule. This is not the place or the time to—"

It had been too exhausting a morning. "Please be quiet," I snapped. "My business is not with you."

The old gentleman waved a hand, dismissing the woman. "Mr. Tomkins, I am aware of the problem," he said quietly. "I'm going to see you and your client as planned. Excuse me. I must get this done." He disappeared through one of the mahogany doors.

Although I felt better, I wasn't sure just why. He hadn't said it was all right, he'd only said he was aware of the problem. But he did say he would see me, and he looked to be a man of his word.

We sat in his corner office looking out over the beautiful coastal mountain range of British Columbia.

"Mr. Tomkins I'm going to speak to Mr. Ortega in Spanish. You speak Spanish, of course?"

"Si." I cleared my throat and hoped I'd said it right.

"We'll go slowly, so that you won't miss anything. All right with you?"

For the next ten minutes I was immersed in a barrage of Spanish. I attempted to look interested and informed. My technique for accomplishing this was simplicity itself: I looked at whoever was speaking, nodding my head sagely whenever there was a pause.

At last it was over. Mr. Nabors leaned back in his leather chair. "Well, that does it. I have no more questions for Mr. Ortega," he said in English. "Why don't you wait outside, Mr. Ortega, and I'll have a word with your attorney."

Here it comes, I thought. Ass-chewing time. Something about this silver-haired gentleman reminded me of my childhood idea of God.

He nodded companionably at me. "You prepared this file very well, young man—very thoroughly. Nicely done indeed.

Not too many attorneys take the time to do it right. You do many of these?"

"Not too many," I said casually.

"This is a very specialized field, and if I may be honest, it doesn't seem to attract an abundance of competent attorneys. Scares them off, I guess. Yes, this file was nicely done."

"Thank you, sir."

"I'm not saying this to make you feel good. I'm selfish. If I can get some good people doing immigration work it would make my job easier. So if you decide to get involved in the field in a larger way, please give me a call and I'll do all I can to assist you."

"I certainly appreciate that, sir. About the originals. Do you want—"

"No. I don't need the damn things. If the copies were suspect I'd need to see them, but these are fine. You know, in Los Angeles, one out of every five applicants is rejected for fraud." He shook his head. "One out of five." He stood, extending his hand. "Give me a call if I can help, Mike."

I felt like hugging the guy.

It was twelve noon and I was safe, but I had to hurry and cancel the "courier." I walked into the British Petroleum office, waving to Ronnie as I passed her. She looked worried.

I dialed the office number. On the third ring, a very angry British Petroleum honcho sprinted into the room. "Who the hell are you?" He made shooing gestures toward the door. "Get the hell out of here. You have quite a nerve."

"Just a minute." I rose to my full height of five feet nine inches, knowing that the best defense is a good offense. "I'm sorry if I inconvenienced you, which I doubt, but—"

"Get out of here or I'm calling the police right now." His face was dangerously red.

From the telephone receiver I could hear Jean's voice, tiny and faraway sounding. I replaced the receiver and edged around the man. "I'm going, I'm going. Let me tell you this,"

I said, from the relative safety of the stairwell door, "you have one hell of a lousy security system if I can do what I did." The door banged shut behind me and I ran down the stairs.

By the time I could get to the phone in the other building, it would be too late for Jean to stop Sue Arnold from catching the flight.

Oh well, I thought, as I entered the waiting area, let her enjoy the flight at my expense. I'd consider it my contribution to the arts.

Paulo stood, searching my face for some sign of how things stood. He broke into a wide grin at my thumbs-up gesture.

"Come on, Paulo," I said. "I'll buy you your first lunch as an almost-American."

Chapter 10

Sonny Branch was a small-town boy who'd made good. At least it appeared that way to the folks in Eudora, Texas. Why, whenever Sonny came home to visit his widowed mama, he sported city clothes made to measure and a pinkie ring set with a ruby big enough to choke a rattlesnake.

He was a good ol' boy, all right. Some thought he'd made his money selling storm windows up north. Others said he'd married a city girl with money. No matter, Eudora was proud of Sonny Branch. If there were those who remembered his scrapes with the law in high school and said he was no better than he should be, there were still more high-minded folks who were ready to say that was just sour grapes.

The truth would have proved everyone right: He *had* made good, and he was no better than he should be.

Sonny Branch was a con artist, one of the best in the business. He had made good at his chosen profession until he got caught in Seattle. I was to learn of his origins later. He had heard of me, and that was enough to cause him to give me a call when his luck ran out and he found himself in the county jail.

"This is a real charmer, Michael," Jean said, announcing the call. "It sounds like he's calling from jail, though."

I went to see him right away.

He was big—over six feet and weighing close to two fifty. The chair groaned as he lowered himself into it in the jail's visiting room. "Take a seat, Mike," he boomed, as if inviting me to take my ease on the back porch after supper.

He looked to be about thirty, with an open, engaging face surmounted by carefully combed brown hair. Even though he'd spent the night as a guest of the county, his clothing was immaculate—from the white-on-white silk shirt and string tie to the glossy tan leather boots.

I liked him immediately. I don't know if I trusted him, but I supposed that under different circumstances I might have. Many people had.

It turned out that Branch and one other individual traveled around the country, engaging in the business of separating other people from their savings.

There are many types of con games. The one Branch preferred was both simple and complex. The pair would go to a shopping center and wait for an older man to get out of a later model car and go into a branch bank.

When the older man came from the bank, the partner, Randolph—an "uneducated" black man—would approach Branch, standing on the sidewalk, and introduce himself within earshot of the mark. He wanted to know where to spend the night, he'd say. He was looking for some action. Could Branch help?

Branch loudly asserts that he isn't from this town himself. At this point Randolph would pull an enormous wad of money from his pocket and explain that he had come from Mississippi that very day and wanted to have some fun.

The next moment was the most important, Branch explained to me. "You have to get their greed working for you," he explained earnestly. He'd pull the old man over, getting him involved, and say to Randolph, "Hey, you'd better put that money in the bank." Turning to the older man, "Ain't that right?"

It would become apparent that the black man doesn't trust banks, will keep the money on him, thank you, and he just wants to spend it all that night on wine, women, and song.

Branch would then take the older man out of earshot of Randolph and conspiratorially suggest that if the "dumb nigger" is bent on squandering his no doubt ill-gotten wealth, they might as well help him get rid of it. Winking at the older man, he suggests a friendly game of poker.

They go to a motel and play cards, the black man always losing. Randolph doesn't protest, but insists that he wants to know that, had he won, he would have been paid. He doesn't mind losing, he says, but wants assurance that Branch and the older man would have paid their gambling debts as honorably as he will do.

After an initial show of hesitation, Branch agrees to this, subtly shaming the mark into going along. The trio takes a ride back to the old man's bank in the shopping center, where the mark withdraws five or ten thousand dollars.

Branch puts the money in a paper bag, and the bag in the trunk of the man's car "for safekeeping." Branch and the black man leave, ostensibly to go to Branch's bank.

The older man eventually tires of waiting for their return. When he opens the paper bag, lo and behold, he discovers that the bag containing what he was certain was his money is in fact full of neatly tied bundles of newspaper.

This scam worked very well around the country, unbelievable as it seems, and Branch had earned his living traveling from state to state, small town to large city, plying his peculiar trade. Last year's gross for his two-man team was $50,000 per person, but, as he explained, his business expenses were necessarily high and he needed large grosses to net fifty thousand.

I took out my yellow pad. "How the hell did you get caught—and where's the money?"

He laughed softly. "It's the damnedest thing. You see, Mike, I had me another partner before this here one, guy by the name of Buck. Last year we came through here. Did pretty good, too. Anyways, Buck, he went down to South Carolina—he was from there—and blew all his money." He shook his head. "Then he got stupid and greedy. Got busted in a burglary down there and the bunco up here."

"Did this Buck guy know if and when you were planning to come back here?"

" 'Course he did. This is one great little town you got here. I'm sure the cops knew I was on my way back, too, and was looking for me."

"Okay. So how'd you actually get caught?"

"Piss poor timing, Mike, just piss poor. Mr. Sanders—guy we took for eleven thousand—well, he apparently called the cops twenty minutes after we left him." He shook his head. "I'd figgered him for a better sport than that. Anyways, we was heading out to the airport to beat feet out of here. Me and Randolph. We get the first plane heading somewheres—anywheres, it don't matter—so we're walking down the concourse. It's not real crowded that day, and I see all these crew-cutted fellers. I say to myself, 'Sonny,' I says, 'you appear to be heading into a little difficulty.' So I turn around and start heading out the way I came in."

"Where was your partner?"

"We didn't walk together. He was behind me. Anyways, I get real close to the door there, and I hear the old 'Stop or you're gonna have to crawl to the door' thing, you know? So I stop. I stop like a Mack truck."

"Who had the money?"

"He did. Randolph. A nice bundle this time, too."

"Where was he by then?"

"Ol' Randolph—faster and smarter. About twenty feet behind me, with a satchel of money. All of it—goddammit—all of it."

"Did they ever catch him?"

"Not so's you'd notice."

"Jesus, Sonny. That's quite a story."

"Ain't it though?" He looked pleased. "What's your thinking on how to get rid of it?"

"Well, we've got a problem," I said slowly.

"I know that. But I got a couple ideas how we can work this

little thing out." He leaned forward, the chair protesting under his bulk. "How much juice we gonna need?"

"Juice?" I asked stupidly.

"Yeah, juice. How much we need to spring me?"

"I don't think you understand, Sonny. This is a—"

"Bullshit, Mike. You just talk to that judge alone, and—"

"Talk to the judge alone? Are you crazy? I'm not allowed to talk to the judge alone—without the prosecuting attorney there—about anything but the weather. It doesn't work that way here, Sonny."

He let his chair fall back and grunted in disgust. "Well, what you gonna do?"

"Hmm . . ." I tapped my pen against my pad. "I think it might work if we can get you the same judge who sentenced Buck."

Sonny brightened. "He good on bunco?"

"I don't know about that," I said absently, "but bet he'd be great on equity. Same crime, after all—even if it is a year and a half later." It sounded good. The argument could be made that the same judge should sentence defendants for the same crime. I didn't really expect that arranging to get Sonny in front of Judge Schaefer for sentencing would be much of a problem. Then I remembered. "Goddammit."

"Uh-oh. I hear that 'goddammit' from a lawyer and I reckon that's as scarifyin' as a doctor sayin' 'Hmmm.' What's the problem?"

"No big deal, Sonny," I said. "But Judge Schaefer is going to retire from the bench in three weeks. If we hurry, that will make it even better. You agree to plead guilty, we get Judge Schaefer for sentencing. We'll try to make it on the very last day he's wearing the black robe. That way, he's not worried about anything, like the press giving him a bad time. He sentenced Buck to a year. In fairness, he should do the same for you."

"Sounds okay to me, Mike." Branch sighed gustily. "You sure you couldn't just talk to him, though?"

"Not in this state, Sonny. This ain't like Texas, I guess."

"I suppose not," he said gloomily. Then he brightened. "You don't have to worry about what I'll do when I'm out. Getting a job is no problem. Pick an area—I have friends everywhere."

"And I'll bet you have enemies everywhere, too," I said sourly. "Con everybody else, Sonny—but not me. Okay?"

There had been five Seattle victims. Branch and Randolph had taken each for between five and eleven thousand dollars apiece for a grand total of $73,000. I could see why Branch held this city in so high a regard.

If I were a victim, I reasoned, I would much prefer to have Branch out and working so as to repay me, than in prison. I called the victims, getting through to three of them. Two agreed with me, grudgingly. The other hung up shortly after I introduced myself.

I was picking up the phone to dial again, when Jean buzzed. "Sam Vickers on two, Michael. Calling about Branch."

"Hi, Sam. What's your recommendation going to be?"

"Ten years."

"Ten years? Ten *years*?" My voice edged toward an upper register. I consciously lowered it. "Why so heavy? This isn't a crime of violence, after all."

"I consider this to be a murder." There was no hint of levity in his voice.

"Come on, Sam. We're not in court here. No need to be theatrical—"

"Mr. Sanders jumped off the Aurora Bridge early this morning. He's dead." Sam cleared his throat. "I suggest that you do not contact his widow."

That did not please me. In addition to the human tragedy, the news about poor Mr. Sanders complicated everything. I wondered how Branch would react to the news. He was a charmer, all right, and I liked him. But then, charm was his stock-in-trade, his inventory. In the way that burglars tend to have tattoos, con artists tend to be nice folks.

The problem with Sonny, though, as I saw it, was that he was too proud of what he'd done, too ready to laugh at the vulnerability of others.

I'd done all I could do. Judge Schaefer would be sentencing Sonny Branch, and it was the last judicial act he would perform. With the suicide of one of the victims following so closely on the heels of the crime, though, I worried that Judge Schaefer might identify too closely with the retired victims.

On the other hand, the press had been grappling lately with the problem of disparate sentencing. Two burglars, in different parts of the city, commit the same crime. One of them is sentenced to six months, and the other is made to serve ten years.

Judge Schaefer had sentenced Buck, who committed the same crime, to one year, as I intended to remind him, and in fairness could not be more harsh with Sonny. I hoped.

On the sentencing date, Branch looked perfect. He absolutely radiated sincerity and repentance. He listened respectfully as the prosecutor made his pitch, and lowered his head in shame at the enumeration of his assaults on the credulity of gullible retired citizens.

I went to work. "Your Honor," I began softly. "Sonny Branch is bright and sensitive, or he couldn't have done what he did, or be so conscience-stricken now. He knows that the stakes are too high to continue that way of life. I ask you for one year—one year, your honor—so that when Sonny Branch has served his time and paid his debt to society he may go to work to repay his debt to the people he has harmed." I sincerely hoped the widow was not present in the courtroom that day. "Your Honor," I continued, louder now, "you sentenced Mr. Branch's partner to one year for the same crime. You will leave the bench and have no regrets in your retirement if you make it possible for Mr. Branch to make retribution." I gestured toward Sonny.

He was sitting erect now, and I noticed with no small measure of irritation that the eyes he directed pleadingly toward Judge Schaefer appeared to glisten with tears.

The prosecutor was going crazy, of course. "Your Honor," he said urgently, "you can't have it both ways."

"Mr. Branch's partner received from you a sentence of one year, your Honor," I repeated. "Therefore, I urge you to make your last judicial act consistent as well as compassionate."

"Okay, Sonny," I said afterward, "I want another five hundred."

"Well, I tell you, Mike, I'm commencing to believe you're just about worth it. So I put it in the mail yesterday." He extended his hand. "I surely do thank you."

I shook his hand. "Never con your lawyer, Sonny. Don't tell me it's in the mail."

He laughed, a good laugh from deep in his belly. "You don't trust me, after all we've been through together?"

I didn't answer.

He shrugged, pulled out his checkbook, wrote the check with a flourish.

Four days later, the damn thing bounced.

Chapter 11

I'd brought Prosser to work with me on the bright autumn morning when Leland Ellis called. "He'd like you to meet him after work for a drink at that little place next to the IBM building. I said you were in conference and would call back," Jean told me. "He didn't have time to hold for you."

"Sure, call and leave a message that I'll be there," I said, reflecting a bit guiltily that I hadn't seen Leland in months.

Prosser followed Jean into the reception room. I waited. Sure enough, within seconds came the sound of Jean's desk drawer being opened softly, followed by the slurping sound of Prosser enjoying a forbidden goodie.

"Jean," I called, "Judith will have my hide if that dog puts on another ounce."

"You, Michael, are an unbelievable fussbudget," Jean answered. "How many calories could there be in one little gumdrop?" I heard Prosser's contented moan as he dropped to her feet for a nap. "I'll take him home with me tonight and you can pick him up after dinner. I'd love to have him."

The bar was crowded at five-thirty, but thick burgundy carpeting hushed the noise of conversation—the little and big deals swirling about. I spotted him at a corner table. Two glasses, already emptied, stood on the small table in front of him, and his hand was raised to signal the waiter.

Leland was not pleased about something, and his tense invitation of the morning suddenly made a lot of sense.

I dropped into the chair opposite him. "Need a priest or a **150** lawyer? Hi, Leland. You look like a bus hit you full on."

"Mike. Good of you to come. Yeah, maybe I do need both. Can we talk—just talk at this point? I have a lot of thoughts that keep bouncing around. Start your meter—this is probably business."

"You keep buying the drinks, I keep the meter off."

We sat in silence after ordering. He fiddled with the black swizzle stick.

"Scottie?"

"Obvious, huh?"

"I hoped not, but like a doctor, I see signs. Is it serious?"

"I guess. I've moved out. The tension wasn't good for the kids. Or us. We've talked, but she doesn't want to keep it together. To be honest, I didn't even know the problem was bad. I mean, fights, sure. I thought they were spats. Maybe that's more indicative of the situation, not knowing how Scottie felt. I mean, how deeply she felt."

"Maybe time away from each other—"

"That's just the problem—too much time away from her. Business meetings, business dinners, weekends at the office. Shit, Mike, you know all this is pretty typical, right? Hell, I thought she wanted the same things I did, so I worked hard to give them to her and the kids."

I didn't say anything. Leland was a junior partner in a small yet very aggressive brokerage firm, specializing in municipal bonds. He had started with them right out of college and never left. Leland worked hard and was succeeding in his climb up the corporate ladder.

I am not a marriage counselor, shrink, or social worker. Some attorneys feel they should be. They feel they have a duty to "help" their clients in nonlegal ways. I am not trained in those professions, and I would be wasting my clients' money or my time delving into areas that are none of my business. My job is to suggest a marriage counselor, shrink, or whatever, when appropriate.

A certain percentage of couples will reconcile with or without my help. Most won't. By the time my phone rings, a decision has been reached. Oftentimes, people want me to tell them they're doing the right thing. "Yeah, he sounds like a real bastard—let's get you divorced." I'll say things if I think my new client needs it, so that his or her recital of the facts and problems will continue to flow, and to let it be known I'm on their side. By no means is this therapy or really helpful to the person. In Leland's case, it was not appropriate, nor would it have been helpful.

"The fact is, Mike," Leland said, "I love to work. Scottie wanted me on a more regular schedule and she . . . well, I guess she got lonely."

"Another man?"

"Absolutely not. No other lady, either. Scottie enrolled in City College just at the time that my work load increased. I've been getting home late, working some on the weekends and soon I wasn't being sensitive to *her* needs. I don't know, maybe she felt some resentment when she quit school to marry me. She thinks she's a coed again—the whole damn family's in school."

"How old are Ron and Debbie now?"

"Eleven and nine. Good kids. Scottie's a good mother, although she's spending more time away from the kids, which I'm not pleased about. You don't need grounds anymore, do you?"

"No, Leland. If Scottie wants a dissolution, she can get one. There no longer is a fault situation, or a bad person. In some states, it still exists, but not here in Washington."

"No more pictures in motel rooms?"

I smiled. "Not for a long time. Much more civilized now."

Leland sipped at his drink. "Well, what do I do now?"

"I assume this procedure will be agreed to? I mean, friendly?"

"I hope so. Hell, if she wants out, fine. I don't see any reason to put the kids in the middle. But Scottie has been up tight lately. We haven't been communicating very well about the division of property. She's suspicious, I guess."

"Has she been to see an attorney?"

"I don't know. I think she saw someone, but that's just a feeling."

"You wouldn't know which one?"

"No, but I think she's looking for a female. She has this thing about men recently—sort of distrustful, like I betrayed her or something, and now she can only trust women. Listen, Mike, I want to be fair, but I've got to live also. I'm paying two twenty a month for this one-bedroom apartment. Christ, our house payment is only two-eighty, and it's a nice home—four bedrooms, view of the sound, a deck I built myself."

"I bet you bought it in 1969 or 1970."

"Yeah, spring of seventy."

"Paid twenty-eight to thirty?"

"Thirty-one, nine five."

"It's probably worth seventy-five to eighty now."

"I know, inflation and all, but—"

"Maybe more. We'll have to get it appraised if it comes to that."

"That's a lot of equity sitting there. I wonder what the lake place is worth. We bought it in 1976. Building a little cabin."

"This is not the time or the place to talk specifics. Call me at the end of the week. Meanwhile, sit down and talk to Scottie, see how far your thinking is apart on money matters. Maybe we don't have to make a big production out of it."

"Okay. I appreciate your just talking like this. Like I said, I'm pretty confused and—hell, I'm insecure myself."

"Leland, listen. You're going to feel guilty no matter what you do, so just accept it. Scottie is a bright, attractive woman. I don't know her very well, but from what you've told me, she's a good mother. What I'll attempt to do is get this matter over with as cheaply and expeditiously as possible. But to do this, both parties have to cooperate."

"Mike, after a period of time, I'm sure Scottie and I can agree on the big issues. As I said before, I don't want a bloodbath."

"Good. Okay, Leland. Get back to me and see if you have any more information. I'd like to keep you and Scottie friends when this is over. There's a lot there to save."

"I'm glad you feel that way, too."

"You coming?" I asked, as I gathered my things.

"No, I'm going to sit here and have one more, and then probably go back to the office and finish off some paper work."

Ten days later, I got a call from Leland. Since he hadn't called earlier, I sort of thought maybe talking about the division of property might have triggered a better atmosphere to explore all the reasons they should stay together. Not so.

"Mike, I'm really pissed. No, actually, I'm furious. I've never been so mad."

"Does that mean you're not pleased, Leland?"

He chuckled a little and calmed down. "Some pimply-faced asshole just walked into my office—my goddamn office, Mike—and served me with papers, a Summons and Petition for Dissolution. Goddammit—"

"Hold on. Just relax. That's nothing out of the ordinary." Actually, I was a little surprised myself. It's pretty unusual that an attorney would be so insensitive as to serve an opposing party in his place of business. I never do that unless I have no other address for the individual—at which point I usually call the individual and tell him that I want to avoid any embarrassment, and would he come in to the office or provide me with an address. Obviously, this is not done in all lawsuits, but in dissolution cases, especially, I feel that cooperation between the parties will facilitate settling the matter. In other words, serving somebody at work gets things officially rolling on a very bad note indeed.

"Uh, Leland, who's handling Scottie's divorce?"

"Shit, I don't know—"

"Look in the lower right-hand corner of the Petition. The attorney's name should be printed on the pleading paper."

"Nelson and Nelson."

"Oh, damn."

"Shit, Tomkins, that was professionally tactful. Not good, huh?"

"No, no, Leland. I was just kidding."

"Like hell. Bad, huh?"

"What do you mean, bad? No, I've had other matters with Nelson and Nelson. No, I was thinking of something else—just reading a memo here."

"You're a terrible liar."

"Who cares about *her* lawyers anyway? There's just not much to argue about, is there? You're agreed on most things, right?"

"No."

"Oh."

"Yeah, oh. We agreed on most things, but she still wanted to have some person—some counsel—to make sure she was getting a square deal. I don't begrudge her that—she needs her own professional—but I resent her doing it anyway. Now you tell me she went to a divorce bomber. Please—the truth, Mike."

"Well, divorce bomber is a bit strong. The Nelson firm does have a reputation for going to the wall with their clients. Very loyal, actually."

"Going to the wall? Be clear, dammit."

"Okay. Not giving an inch—sucking every advantage out of a situation. They're a good firm, expensive. To be honest, Leland, my experience is that very few couples end up friends when the Nelson firm gets involved. Let me tell you a story. A friend of mine, a young lawyer, was having marital problems. They didn't want to finalize a dissolution, so they drafted a separation agreement dividing up the debts and property. This guy was worried, though, that if a divorce was finally decided on by either one of the parties, and it got a little sticky, that Nelson and Nelson would get involved. They both agreed that no one would use the Nelson firm, and actually put it into the separation agreement. My friend felt that if his wife went to them, well, it would end up a bloody, unnecessarily messy thing."

"Super. Now she's got them, what's next?"

"Send me the papers. We have twenty days to put in an answer to her petition. But before that, I'll file a notice of appearance telling her attorney I'm involved."

"Mike, I don't want to fight with Scottie, but Jesus—she wants everything. Custody, the house, my pension, maintenance, four hundred dollars a month child support, and she wants me to pay her attorney's fees. The more I read the paper, the madder I get."

"Leland, don't worry about the piece of paper. That's just the opening shot. Boiler-plate language. It's mostly form, not much substance. Listen, Leland, don't talk to Scottie about anything substantive, okay? Just say that the lawyers should do the talking. Don't stop communicating, just don't speak about any of the major issues—even though you want to. And don't talk to her if you can't control your temper. There's no advantage in getting into a yelling match. I'll send you copies of the answer, which will basically say the same thing her petition does, but saying you get most of it—and of course less money for child support and maintenance. Okay, now let me do the worrying for you. The real negotiations are some time away."

Within two weeks, I'd put in my answer and cross petition. My phone calls established that Scottie believed that Leland was making a great deal of money, and, since she had limited job skills, Leland was going to have to support his family and Scottie until such time as she was able to take care of her responsibilities.

"I'll be sending over our standard Interrogatories, along with a Motion to Show Cause for Temporary Child Support, Temporary Maintenance and Temporary Attorney's Fees. Scottie is without funds to litigate the issues."

Ms. Nelson was probably sixty years old. She had graduated law school when a woman was literally never even seen in a law school, except to swab down the floors at night. To call her a tough old bird would be too gentle. She fights like hell for her clients, knows it all, and is very good. She puts *her* firm's reputation on the line in *every* case. There usually is no easy case with her firm, and every step is a struggle. All *i*'s and *t*'s must be dotted and crossed or she'll crucify you.

"Your standard Interrogatories, Ms. Nelson, as I remember them, are eighty-two pages long and contain two hundred twenty-five questions about the first penny he made—beginning with the paper route Leland had when he was ten."

"Yes, Mr. Tomkins, they are complete."

"What are you going to ask for in the way of temporary support during the pendency of this action?"

"That, of course, will depend on the answers to the financial questions. But assuming Leland makes around thirty-two thousand, we feel six hundred dollars temporary maintenance and two hundred fifty per child per month, plus two hundred temporary attorney's fees is a fair amount. He should also keep the mortgage current."

"The figures you state are fairly accurate, but I can't agree with the conclusion. Leland has to support himself too, and what you're asking for, after deductions, is not going to be easy to manage."

"I'm sure he'll find a way, Mr. Tomkins. Most men do."

"Well, I think your motion is out of line, but send me the papers and I'll discuss it with my client. If I have a counterproposal that you might accept, I'll call to see if we can draft an agreed order rather than go on the Family Law Calendar."

The Family Law Calendar is a special courtroom that is set aside, beginning at 1:30 P.M. every day, to hear a plethora of motions concerning "family law." Much of the daily calendar is taken up with motions for temporary orders, which means that the sitting judge is asked to decide how much support money should be paid until the dissolution is finally granted—anywhere between sixty days or six months if a full trial is needed.

Motions for temporary maintenance—support for the wife, which is different from temporary child support—are argued before the judge based on affidavits submitted to the court by the parties. In a case like this, the female party states that she is starving, has no money, can't feed the little ones, can't find a job, has no job skills, can't pay the mortgage—oh, woe is me. The man states that his job is tenuous, what with layoffs, there is no more overtime like last year, and that last year's 1040 tax form is no longer relevant; that all his wife wants the money for is to buy new clothes so she can go out—not to look for a job, but to party.

The judge has about seven or ten minutes to hear these lies, half-truths, and overstatements. He then has to make substantial monetary decisions, as well as decisions about visitation, temporary custody, etc. It is not an enviable task for anyone.

The courtroom is crowded with attorneys milling about, getting bored waiting for their minutes before the judge. Most of the time, the clients do not come to hear the arguments, as no testimony is taken, but occasionally the client shows up to make sure that his attorney squeezes every drop of blood from the opposing turnip. It's a really fun time for all.

Attorneys try to avoid going on that calendar. I knew I couldn't avoid it on this case.

"Well, Leland, I've got bad news and bad news. Which do you want first?"

"Give me the good news first."

"Are you deaf, too? I don't *have* any good news. The judge said that based on your projected income, temporary child support was ordered in the amount of $175 per kid—which isn't too bad—and temporary maintenance in the amount of

$300 per month; you pay the mortgage and $150 suit money. Visitation wasn't an issue, since you and Scottie said there was no problem in that area."

"It's not as bad as you led me to believe it could have been, but it seems a little excessive."

"Now remember, Leland, this is all temporary—just like the name—and almost without exception, all the money is less when the final decree is entered."

"If that's the case, why should the wife ever negotiate—just stall until a trial?"

"A good question. To be honest, when I've represented the wife in the past and I made out like a bandit for temporary support, I've stalled like hell. You've got the hammer in negotiations."

"Whatever happened to Women's Lib? They want to be independent—freedom and all that. Now they scream and cry 'Give me, support me.' Shit."

"Be that as it may, the temporary order reads 'Payments to be made on the first and the fifteenth of the month,' so in six days give Scottie a half payment."

"You know, Mike, I don't think I like her very much anymore."

After the flurry of activity, and after the Interrogatories were answered, things settled down until I got a call from Doris Nelson, telling me that Leland was not prompt with his support payments and that I had better speak to him. "I don't want to go back to court for a contempt of court hearing."

Then I got a call from Leland telling me that he'd heard from his kids that Scottie was dating this college professor and he was damn sure she was sleeping with him and he was damn well not going to pay her to "fuck around."

"She's taking some classes at the university and she's, uh, dating this guy. So I went over to the house to see the kids and give her the damn check—"

"Did you call first, or just come over?"

"No, the kids said to just come over. Hell, it's my house, isn't it? I pay for it. I don't have to call to see my kids or Scottie."

"You still have your key?"

"Absolutely. It's my house, and I still have tools and other things I need to get to from time to time."

"Leland, I told you not to antagonize Scottie. For Christ's sake, lie low. My job is hard enough, what with you the male, the Nelson firm—give me some help so I can negotiate this thing and not have to slug it out in court."

Soon after that discussion with Leland, I received an Order to Show Cause why Leland should not be restrained from phoning, molesting, visiting, communicating, harassing or any other thing, Scottie. As I suspected, Leland's impetuous (if not planned) foray into his old haunt was going to cost me a trip to court. I'm sure Scottie was angry about having her privacy invaded, and I was further sure that Nelson was fanning the anger. Settlement—even the prospect of it—was fast fading as a hope.

A restraining order is usually sought by one side when violence has occurred or is likely to occur. It is not uncommon that one party will attempt to annoy the other party through a smack on the mouth during private negotiations, or calling late at night and speaking in a rather forceful voice, "You bitch, you're not going to get a dime from me. I'll quit my *job* before I give you one lousy cent, you ugly prune." Such conversation is usually detrimental to the settlement attempts of the respective attorneys.

I was not pleased that Scottie thought that she needed this "paper protection." Clients have asked me how a piece of paper will protect them after the other party has made it clear that he wishes to rearrange their teeth. "Am I supposed to hold up this piece of paper like a curse against a werewolf and stop his fist?"

What actually happens is that when a restraining order is signed by the court, the attorney gets a certified copy of the original and presents it to the client. If the terms of the order are broken, then the police can be called. If the husband, for instance, comes barging into his wife's house, the police, after perusing the certified copy of the order, order him to leave her alone. If he does not, they may then haul him away. Without a court order, the police are powerless to do anything if no violence has occurred. After all, the gentleman is legally standing in his own house, screaming at his own wife, and probably breaking his own vases and glasses.

He will be calmed down by the police and if that doesn't work, they will ask him to leave. Legally, though, this will be a suggestion. Police love these kinds of situations, since everyone is walking and reacting in this gray area. The police usually leave the scene as soon as possible to take their dinner break.

For this reason, restraining orders are rather common in dissolution cases.

In Leland's case, since violence was not a possibility, and I didn't feel it would in any way jeopardize our position, I agreed to mutual restraining orders, meaning both parties would be restrained from doing the same things to one another.

Things were relatively quiet after this round of sparring. Leland took the kids on the weekends with some regularity. Scottie, I heard, was dating around and experiencing life as a student and as a single parent.

Nelson and I were getting the house appraised, evaluating Leland's pension rights with his company, and trying to figure out what we could and could not agree on.

Nelson wouldn't give an inch, and each concession was hard won. But if we couldn't agree on the total package, all the prior agreements would be for naught.

Despite the painful arm wrestling, things were progressing slowly, but they were progressing. Until I got a call from Leland at seven-thirty one Sunday morning.

"You're going to be pissed off, Mike."

"I doubt it could be any more than I am now. It's seven-thirty. I don't even have seven-thirty on my watch. Well?"

"I saw Scottie at a party last night."

"You dating now?"

"I didn't take her, Mike. I didn't even know she was going to be there. Anyway, Scottie was with Joe College and I was with Joanne Walker—"

"Uh-oh."

"Yeah. Well, anyway, Scottie went to the bathroom and we, uh, talked—said some things we shouldn't have. Well, I kind of goaded her until she said—"

"I don't care about the conversation, jerk. What happened? This isn't 'Meet the Press.' "

"I . . . well, I smacked her."

"Jesus Christ."

"It was real tacky. Yelling. The party was sort of ruined."

"What did Joe College do?"

"Well, he was really cool about everything. Suggested I leave, actually."

"Good advice. Higher education must be—never mind. Did you leave?"

"Yeah."

"Open hand or fist?"

"Shit, Mike, what kind of person—well, open hand, of course."

"Damage?"

"My ego, self-esteem—"

"I mean to Scottie."

"I've never hit a woman before."

"Was she hurt?"

"Shit, I feel terrible. Booze, anger, seeing her with a date—I just flipped out."

"Was she hurt, you ass?" I was insistent this time.

"No, not really. It was a quick slap."

"Did she hit you back, at least?"

"Scottie? Hit back? No, she's too classy to do that. Besides, it hurt more by her not doing anything. Listen, I feel like a snake. What's this going to do to the, uh—"

"Guess."

"Well, I'm going to get some sleep. I just wanted to talk to you and, uh, I'll call you."

"Monday. Make it Monday."

"Hey, I'm sorry. I just needed to talk."

"Okay. No sweat. I was just reading the advance sheets anyway. Get some sleep, Leland. I'll talk to you tomorrow."

Leland didn't call on Monday. In fact, I didn't hear from him until the end of the week. He sounded down and confused.

"Mike, I've done a lot of thinking. And, besides feeling like an ass, I've come to some general conclusions."

"Go on." I sounded wary, I guess, because I had a pretty good idea of what was coming.

"I don't want to go to trial. That's clear. I don't want to put Scottie through that and, hell, I don't want to put me through that either. It's going to cost money and what would I gain—a little break on maintenance, maybe child support. Hell, she's going to get the big stuff—furniture and all that. Anyway—"

"Well, now you're talking in degrees. It will be more expensive, Leland, and take longer too. Trial is now set for five months from now. Listen, Leland, is this guilt because you hit Scottie?"

"Sure, partially."

"Let's wait. I don't want to cave in because you got loaded at a party and sort of blew it one time. I think you could do better at trial rather than arm wrestle with Nelson for all of it."

"I want this thing over with as soon as possible. I'm not going to change my mind. This limbo is driving me crazy. The kids are acting strange toward me. Shit. Scottie is sleeping with that jerk in front of *my* kids. I want out sooner than later. Make the best deal you can for me and punt. No trial."

"You sure?"

"Yeah. I wanted to be friends when this thing started and still do. We won't if we continue this circus. Don't totally sell me out. Let me keep my Boy Scout merit badge sash. But screw it. Let her have it all—the new car, the house—I don't care. I'll support her while she's in school until she gets a degree or whatever. Hell, I spent the week working, drinking, and reading *Ms.* magazine. Can you believe that?"

"Leland?"

"Mike, I'm sure. It's not just guilt from the party. Maybe other guilt—who knows?"

No question the process can get to people. The psychological roller coaster can be debilitating. Settling out of court was in this case not a bad thing to do. He may have gotten more at the time of trial, but probably not significantly.

I called Ms. Nelson and explained that for business reasons we wanted to avoid trial, but if we couldn't work it out, I was prepared to go to the mat.

"You know, Mr. Tomkins, your client violated the Restraining Order by harassing and striking my client."

"Well, not exactly. But I feel talking about a situation that will not happen again is not productive."

"Violating a court order is not productive, Mr. Tomkins."

"Ms. Nelson," I said, getting a bit hot, "the Restraining Order never mentioned striking—only verbally abusing, and only at her place of residence. As you know, this incident—regrettable as it was—took place at a location away from your client's home. So why don't you stop posturing and digging in your heels, and begin what is likely to prove a difficult process of dividing up their property?"

It was indeed difficult. The process took three tortuous weeks of phone calls and two meetings, always at Ms. Nelson's office. I was getting my brains beat out, but managing some small property victories. I would confer with Leland daily and inform him how the battle was proceeding.

He would always say, "Fine, fine. I agree. Sure, I'll take care of all medical expenses for the three of them." Or, "Sure, fine—one-hundred-thousand-dollar life insurance policy with the kids as beneficiaries. Of course, go ahead."

And so on. Then it was finally over.

"Well, Leland, I think we have an agreement."

"Good."

"I'll send you a draft of the agreement to look over and we'll fine tune it if you think it's necessary. Then it will be over. Actually, it's not too bad, Leland—hell, you got your golf clubs and one of the ice trays from the freezer."

"Good. I can always use an extra ice tray."

Days later Leland called. He'd had time to look over the first draft of the property settlement agreement.

"Do you think you can get me the other ice tray, Mike? It's a shame to break up the set."

"I'm sure of it, Leland. After all, what am I here for?"

"I guess it's over then. Oh, hey, I'm going to pick up the kids this weekend and I'll probably just take Boris—this time, to keep."

"Boris?"

"Yeah, Boris. My bassett. Scottie gave him to me because I used to wear Hush Puppies a lot. Never had a dog before. But it sure will be comforting to have a pal around the apartment. He looks like I feel."

"Boris, huh?"

"Yeah. I spent a solid week looking for an apartment house that would take pets—gave them a $250 damage deposit and a promise he wouldn't bark. What's the matter, Mike, should he have been mentioned under the custody section?" He laughed in a lighthearted way I'd not heard in some time.

"Okay, then, Leland, I'll call Nelson up and say it's been agreed to."

Ms. Nelson called the following Monday morning. "Mr. Tomkins, you said we had an agreement last Friday, and now your client totally breaches the spirit of that agreement."

"You got the right number, Ms. Nelson? What are you talking about?" But I already knew.

"Your client refuses to return my client's property—Boris."

"Boris?" I shouted. "What the hell are you talking about—Boris?"

"It's not his property."

"Now wait a minute. Are you telling me that Scottie won't give up Boris? I can't believe such bullshit."

"Believe it, Mr. Tomkins." The dry, ladylike voice was as cool as ever.

"Son of a bitch. Well, I suppose you've taken everything else, so you might as well get the goddamn dog, too. I'll call my client. But it's conceivable that since Boris's custody was not contemplated by the agreement . . ." I trailed off.

"Get back to me, please, Mr. Tomkins, with the time that Boris will be returned to my client."

"That insensitive, stupid bitch, that old wrinkled she-wolf. I can't believe she's backing Scottie up on this. What a pair—"

"Well, I don't know, Leland. What do you want to do?"

"Fight, Mike. I mean, till the last dog is hung. We're going to court. She is going to have to fight for everything. No agreements. At all. Period. Finis."

"Good, Leland. I have heard of tasteless—oh, hell. We both feel the same way."

"I mean, Mike, Boris is *mine.* The kids are too busy with baseball and ballet, Scottie has always been totally ambivalent about him even though she got him for me as a gift. I walk him, I feed him, and now—it's Nelson, Mike. It's not Scottie. I know that. I *think* I know that. Anyway, I want Boris and I'm going to get him."

I started to prepare for trial, gathering income tax records, wage slips, pension records—and now, rabies shot records.

Nelson said her client would not budge and she was in total agreement. I asked her if she minded spending her client's money when she knew, as an expensive attorney, that one little word from her to Scottie would resolve the whole thing. "The topic, Mr. Tomkins, is not open for discussion."

Leland came into the office one morning a month before trial. I had not spoken to him in some time—no reason to. I was ready for a two-day trial, and he was pouring himself into his work.

He slouched in the chair, wrinkling the back of his well-tailored tweed sport jacket.

"And you have been . . ."

"Okay, Mike. Dating a little, working my ass off to pay you."

"Good. Like to hear that. You want to say something?"

"I'm embarrassed."

"You didn't hit her again, did you?"

"No, no. Nothing like that. Uh, well, I want Boris to stay with Scottie."

"Okay, what happened?"

"Well, I'd gotten drunk after a late meeting with some regional managers. Day before yesterday, it was. I had started talking to this guy who was recently divorced himself. We started feeding on each other and drinking, getting more and more angry.

"So I got up from the table and drove over to the house. I was going to tell Scottie just what I thought of her, what she was doing to me and the kids—just cleanse my soul. I knew I probably was going to get in trouble for going over to the house except to pick up the kids."

"Yep, you are," I said.

"So, I pulled up to the house, slammed the car door, and stalked up to pound on the front door. Just as I started to lift my arm, I looked into the living room. Scottie was curled up by the fire, hugging her knees in a big caftan thing she has. She was just sitting on the floor stroking Boris and crying. God, Mike, it tore me up. All the fight and anger went out of me."

"So?"

"So, I knocked. And Scottie and I finally talked. Really talked. She was feeling down. We talked about how this all started. I never really knew. I guess I don't truly know now. I just know a little better.

"Anyway, she talked to me and I listened. We drank some wine—even went to bed."

"You've reconciled?"

"No. No, don't worry. She really does like Boris. She says he reminded her of the good old days. She's not that same person. Hell, I'm not that same person. We talked—and it's settled."

"Oh yeah?"

"This time it really is, Mike. I get Boris half time and the kids half time. Scottie and I are—maybe—going to date. After it's final."

I looked at him skeptically. Who the hell knows—maybe it *was* settled.

Months later I saw Leland eating lunch at a corner table, obviously waiting for someone. I tapped him on the shoulder. "Scottie?"

"What?"

"Are you waiting for Scottie—or for some other lady?"

"Nope. A fat, balding bond lawyer from the Bronx. He's boring and his head gleams."

"Sorry I can't stay. How's Scottie? Dating each other?"

"That bitch. I see her every other weekend, when I pick up the kids. What a screaming broad."

"Oh. How's Boris?"

"He looks—well, he looks like you do right now." He smiled a big, broad, toothy grin.

It really was over.

Chapter 12

*I*t had been an amazing year, I thought, as I opened the envelope from Alaska. I hadn't heard from Janet since she'd settled her case and left for Soldotna, Alaska. I'd learned a lot, I reflected, but I still didn't know where Soldotna was.

Dear Mike,

How goes it? I love it up here and am planning on getting married soon. Paul is a super guy. I'll introduce you to each other when we come down to Seattle again.

In the meanwhile, I have a friend who can use your services. He and some other people have a small company which deals in "legal highs." Do you know anything about that? Anyway, they're starting to sell a lot of merchandise and will soon be needing an attorney to help with the business end of thing—and whatever else comes up.

My friend's name is Jack Nolte, and I expect that he will be calling you soon.

Give Prosser my love and the biggest of hugs to both of you.

Love,
Janet

The phrase "legal high" is almost nonsensical. *Legal* and *high*, with a few carefully controlled exceptions, such as alcohol, are mutually exclusive words. Some things, though, are legal, but just barely. State legislators meet every year and always add, rarely delete, laws pertaining to over-the-counter drugs, controlled substances, board of pharmacy rules and regulations.

In other words, what's legal on January first of one year might be illegal on January first of the following year. Especially if it gives you a buzz. So the entrepreneurial chemists go back to their labs in their attic or basement and change a molecular structure here, a chemical bond there, and come up with some powder which is now legal. Until the next session of the legislature.

Then there are the FDA rulings, Product Safety Commission, and other alphabet agencies attempting to protect the public from getting loaded legally.

Jack Nolte called before the week was out. "Janet said you'd be a good guy to see. I'd like to bring my partner over for a little business meeting."

Nolte arrived with his partner, Ralph Raggio. Nolte was clearly the leader and the street smarts of the operation. He was about thirty and bore a remarkable resemblance to a sixties-style hippie. His dirty-blond hair straggled over an orange T-shirt. Raggio was small and tidy, looking like he belonged in the Kingston Trio. He was a graduate of the University of Washington School of Chemistry and was in it for the money, hoping to retire in a few years.

"Is it that profitable?" I asked.

"Oh yeah, man," said Nolte. "It's starting to get really good now, but even last year we made about twenty or thirty thousand apiece, didn't we Ralph?"

Ralph nodded.

"Why is it getting big so fast?"

"We invented this new product that could go very big. It's a kind of incense that has effects like an upper, sort of."

"If you drink it," said Ralph. "It won't do a thing for you if you sniff it or anything."

"You said incense," I reminded Nolte.

"Yeah. We package it that way and advertise it that way—that's one of the reasons we need to talk to you."

It seems that the FDA was attempting to try to block the sale of any such product that implied in advertising or on the package that it was made to be swallowed for the purpose of getting high. There were other problems, too.

"We claimed that it was not a new drug or food and that they had no jurisdiction to issue a Cease and Desist order. That held them for a while, but Ralph and me, we don't have time to handle all that paper work. We need to be out on the road, handling the business with suppliers and distributors and retailers. We don't have the time or the smarts to be dealing all the time with the paper pushers."

They needed an attorney for other things, too. The business should be incorporated, I told them. Incorporation would provide some legal protection against any personal liability. Just like any other business, if theirs was to make it, the owners were going to need help with taxes and other business matters. The IRS would be scrutinizing them very closely, I suggested, the more money they had to admit they earned.

"Can you do all that for us, Mike?" Nolte looked at Ralph, who nodded. "We can bring all our paper work over tomorrow for you to look at."

"I don't know," I said slowly. "I'm not really sure I could do you that much good. Your immediate problem is fighting the FDA. And that's the kind of fight that you can lose by winning. They have unlimited resources, and you don't."

It was clear to me that they needed an attorney, but I wanted to think about it for a while before I leaped in and let them believe it would be me.

After they left, I hung around a while, waiting for Judith. We were going to a party later that evening, and she'd taken a cab downtown to meet me at my office.

"I thought I was past the time in my life when I'd have to weigh a case to see if I was comfortable doing it," I told Jean. "Somehow I thought those sorts of decisions would go away when I got older."

"This . . . incense, or whatever it is that they sell," she said, frowning. "Can it hurt people? Either as an incense or by drinking it as tea?"

"No."

"So what's the problem?"

"It's not just the incense I'm worried about—it's the whole business. They sell things and advertise in publications that make getting high look fun."

"It is, isn't it?" said Jean.

"Yeah, I guess. But kids can buy all this stuff—and maybe kids aren't too bright about how much to take at a time and maybe they could get hurt or die or something."

"Who could die?" asked Judith, breezing in and kissing me hello.

"We're talking about legal highs," Jean told her.

"Oh. Why?"

"Michael might have as clients the owners of a company that deals in things like that."

"You mean like bongs and roach clips and all those little packets of powdered things they sell in head shops?" Judith looked at me. "Mike! Those things can be terribly dangerous, especially to kids."

"But they're not illegal," said Jean thoughtfully.

"I have something of a problem with it," I said, "but no more so than if the owners of a whiskey distilling plant wanted me to represent their business interests."

"That's a dumb comparison," said Judith, beginning to pace. "And you can't compare it to that poor child molester, either. In that case, you just represented him after he'd done a crime, you didn't help him do it."

"What they do is not illegal, Judith," I reminded her.

"Still, people should be protected from things like that, with a potential of hurting somebody."

"I don't know," said Jean, "if people aren't protected a little bit too much already. I'd like to believe that the Constitution guaranteed me the right to make a damn fool of myself and to make a mistake now and again."

"A fatal one?" asked Judith.

"But if you say that strict regulation of each and every thing that might give you a little buzz is the right way to go, where do you draw the line?" I looked at Judith. "Weren't you the one who was telling me about the metabolic effects of sugar? And how it couldn't get approved today if it had just been invented?"

"That's not really what we're talking about, now is it, Michael?" Jean gathered up her coat and prepared to leave. "We're talking about your feelings about taking Nolte and Raggio as clients."

"What do you think?" I watched her turn off the Xerox machine.

"I think you take the case or don't take the case based on your feelings about how you'd get along with the people involved. Does it sound like a good thing for you to do? If so, do it. I don't recall anybody appointing you judge of the whole world," Jean said. "And with that rather pompous evasion, I'm leaving. Good night, Michael. Good night, Judith."

"I think the world of Jean," said Judith when she'd left, "but I disagree with her right now. I think there are more important things to think about than whether or not you're comfortable taking the business as a client."

"Prohibition didn't work, either, Judith," I said, as we prepared to go. "People always look for something to make them high. That's been true of every known civilization."

"Yeah, but somebody has to step in sometimes and say 'hey this stuff could be dangerous.'"

"Maybe so. I'll have to think about it some more."

I never actually made the decision. Not as a decision. I explained the FDA aspect of it to Lamb, who jumped with enthusiasm into researching Nolte's product. When Nolte and Raggio came into the office again, Lamb sat in with us.

That evening, when Jean had gone, Lamb sauntered into my office. "I just want to tell you that I'm not going to participate in this case, or help in any way with it from now on."

"Why?"

He took a chair. "Because I don't like your guy or his problem. And," he tucked his hands in his vest pockets, "there's no reason to work your ass off for no money—absolutely no money. If they really wanted or needed our office, they would have tossed a little of what they made last year toward you."

"They've invested all of that in the new product," I said. "I've asked. There isn't any loose money—"

"Then don't do any work for them."

"Why not? I'm not yet at the point of being busy forty-five hours a week, and therefore I'm not totally maxed out. I'll take a chance on them, throw the dice. Why not? Maybe I'll get some money I wouldn't have gotten otherwise. What's wrong with that?"

"It's not worth it, Tomkins."

"You said that. You're not making sense. You don't like the taking of risks—yet you go to Vegas, or would go to Vegas if you were making the money I make. And without batting an eye you would literally roll the dice and think nothing of it. What the hell is the difference? No flashing lights, no black-stockinged girls, I admit. But no difference, except that if I lose, I lose time, not money. You think I'm a reckless gambler?"

"The biggest one I've seen. You take more flaky pay-on-the-come clients than any attorney I've ever known."

"That's garbage," I said.

"No it's not. I think that without question your no-pay rate is much greater than for anybody else I know."

"I think you're dead wrong. But assuming I take more chances than you would, what's wrong with taking chances? Especially if you know you can afford the dice throw going in?"

"If you don't understand, I don't know how I can explain it to you. It reflects badly on you. You get a reputation for taking clients whom nobody else will take. That in turn attracts flakes, and flakes hang out with flakes. You get more marginal clients, never the substantial clients I want. Playing straight I'll win."

"You mean that in a city like Seattle, a good client won't walk in my door after hearing good things about me because he may also have heard I represent a flake or two?"

"Yes."

"So money from flakes isn't as spendable as money from General Motors or somebody like that?"

"That's not the point, Tomkins."

"Since when is making money not the point of business— and we are in a business, Lamb, whether you like to accept that or not."

"You're right. That is the point. I'm a lawyer and you're a businessman. I practice law—which is not always easy with you around—and you don't. At least not primarily "

"What do you mean, it's not easy with me around."

"I mean your dog hanging around half the time, and your smart-talking secretary, and the parade of scumbags going in and out of here. It makes it hard."

"And you don't approve of the way I practice," I said.

"Nope. I wouldn't put up with the scumbags. It just isn't worth it to me. I'm an attorney. I get paid for my time, to run a case the way I see fit. Why put up with garbage if you don't have to?"

"Money. Why put up with anybody's garbage, if not to make a living? I'm probably not the best attorney around, and I'll never get the high-powered clients. So I'm always going to be taking chances with getting paid and getting a specific result. I think that's what running a small business is all about."

"The big firms don't take chances. There, it's pay or go away."

"I think that's bullshit. I don't think the associates are al-lowed to take chances, but I'd bet my ass the big guys do—and sometimes make big money on them. What the hell is an antitrust case, except a gamble? Three to five years' work and a possibility of a fat loss."

"Substantially different—"

"Why? Because my clients are a little sleazy? Because they wear jeans and are small-time? Big firms represent the manufacturers of Agent Orange. So you think a fat retainer is respectable but a gut feeling and the hope that I'll get paid down the line makes me a sleaze?"

"In a way."

"Perhaps your associating with me may have done damage to your reputation in the community even by this time?"

"I doubt it, you're not very well known." He smiled. "Let's drop it, okay, Mike? We're not getting anywhere talking around in circles."

"No, I don't want to drop it. I want an answer from you." I leaned over my desk. "In other words, it's okay to bend statutory language, play procedural games with an adversary, but if you play games of any kind outside of that carefully defined circle, that's being sleazy rather than being an advocate? A landlord can pay you to evict someone and that's no sweat because you have a nice office and get to keep your emotional distance. But I get involved in my client's affairs and even 'bet' on the outcome by not taking money up front, and that's sleazy?"

"It's just not my style," Lamb said, turning to go into his office.

"And yet," I said quietly, "if I pay you by guessing right on this thing and get paid more than the straight time I've earned because I tack on the sleaze factor—that would be okay?"

"That's human nature," he said from the doorway. "We all do that."

"Is it fair to say that how you appear to people is more important than what you really are?"

He didn't answer.

I didn't want to talk to him anymore that day. Lately life seemed to be one moral dilemma after another, and I was sick and tired of it. It must be comforting to be working for a regular paycheck and have the senior partner of the firm prance in and order you to evict a cripple or defend a company that pours oil into bird sanctuary waters.

I was beginning to envy people like Judith—professionals who had security and prestige and no moral decisions to make about antibiotics. Plus, I was pissed off at John "holier-than-thou" Lamb. The son of a bitch could starve to death with his lousy creased jeans, his lawyers' lawyer attitude. "I'm not a messenger boy," my ass. I fantasized his asking me for money. "John, my good man," I'd say pompously, "I'm not a bank. I'm a sleazy lawyer with money. So please take your clean hands and beg somewhere else." I love to fantasize; I think it's good for the soul. But this time it didn't make me feel any better.

John was right to a point, ungrateful to a larger point. If he had said one more goddamn word about Jean, I would have told him to find his own Katherine Hepburn at thirteen hundred a month to yes sir and no sir him into poverty.

Still angry, hurt, and confused, I arrived home to find Judith emerging from the bathroom, toweling her hair. Prosser didn't bound to greet me, as he usually did. Instead, he sulked in the corner.

"Hi, kid," I said to Judith. "You smell and look delicious. What's with bozo in the corner?" I reached down to rub Prosser's ear.

"Don't pet him, Mike. He's being punished. While I was in the shower he pushed open the door and got the toothpaste from the vanity. He had a sloppy supper of Colgate."

"At least no doggy breath tonight."

Judith wrapped the towel turban fashion around her head. "You okay?"

"Yeah. Well, no—I don't know. Lamb's an ungrateful jerk, I don't know what to do about this legal-high business. You know, I have to keep figuring this out over and over again, whether I'm an amoral greedy bastard, or just a realist trying to pay the rent."

"Want to talk?" She curled up on one corner of the couch, watching me intently.

"I'm just sick and tired of constantly having to take my moral temperature all the time. Does everybody do it, like picking their noses? And they just don't talk about it in public? Or am I turning into Hamlet?"

"I don't think so, Mike. But you know what?" She patted the couch beside her. "You're not a knee-jerk type. You question, ask, probe. It hurts, that's for sure, but I think it needs to be done and I'm proud that you do it. I've learned a lot from you. And about you."

"Aw shucks, doc, it's just a job that's gotta be done."

"Want a medal? A pat on the back?"

"Real bad, yeah."

"Come here," she said, "doctor will fix you up—or anyway, she'll try."

She did.

Some weeks later, at four o'clock on a cold and rainy Tuesday, Jean appeared at my office door. "Sorry to interrupt, Michael, but this is important. You'd better take it."

"Sorry to disturb you, Mike, but we got one bad blowup brewing," Nolte's voice blasted through the receiver. "We just got a call from one of our retailers in Framingham, Massachusetts. A good store, does good business. Well, anyway, one of the employees—some dumb bitch—sold some stuff to a kid."

"How old?" I was taking notes furiously.

"Shit, man, I don't know. I got no information at this point, I just got off the goddamn phone. Cops say the kid is in the hospital and the parents found some stuff in his room."

"Was the retailer arrested?"

"Not yet. But he's up tight. His old lady is knocked up and he don't want to spend no time in cold storage."

"Calm down, Nick." I interrupted his nervous recitation. "Can the store get an attorney?"

"Hey, man," his voice dropped, "they were covering the bills. A lot of our stores are going to be watching to see how we deal with this—how we back up our people. So you drop what you're doing and get down there."

"Nick, it isn't quite that easy." I wrote "Framingham, Massachusetts, reservation asap" on my pad. I didn't have to buzz Jean; she was hovering near the door. "I'd have to rearrange—"

"Hey, Mike, do what you gotta do. No sweat. We don't need this kind of trouble—not now."

"Not ever, Nick." I promised to get back to him when I knew something.

The kid, aged fourteen, was in intensive care, and had been there for thirty-six hours. The parents were middle-class teacher types, who were shocked to come home and find their son comatose. The mother went crazy after finding a lid of grass, a hash pipe, and some incense hidden in the boy's room. The police, after confiscating those things, rousted the legal-high retailer.

"Your reservations are confirmed; you leave at six-fifteen tomorrow afternoon. That should give us time to square things away here," Jean said, reading from a list she held. "You didn't say, but I arranged for a rental car to be waiting at the airport and made an open reservation at the nearest Holiday Inn. I've canceled what I can and should be able to reschedule everything else."

"Thanks."

"What caused the child to overdose, Michael—if that's indeed what happened?"

"No one knows, Jean. Would you put in a call to the hospital. I don't think anybody's going to talk to me, but—"

"It's worth a try," Jean said, turning to go to the phone.

Then I remembered. I was supposed to be meeting Judith at that very moment for a drink. "And Jean, call the Copper Lantern and page—"

"She's coming over here, Michael. I caught her before she left the clinic."

I called Johnny Pignatero, the owner of the retail outlet in Framingham. I advised him to talk to no one until I arrived, and to call my office if he had any information about any of it.

The remainder of that afternoon and most of the following morning were spent piecing together what disparate bits of information I could get and talking to the pharmacists about dosages, symptoms, and reactions.

Then we learned that the child had died at seven that morning and the results of the autopsy would be made available later in the day. The detective assigned to the investigation said he would call me.

He didn't, but Pignatero did. "Not us, Mike," he said, "not even close. The kid died as a result of a diabetic coma. No one knew he was a diabetic and he went on a junk-food binge after smoking grass or some damn thing. Police types are still poking around here—but just to hassle. Business is for shit, but it'll pick up in a few days. Guess I won't be meeting you after all. Say hello to Nick and the guys."

I stared at the phone for a long moment after I'd hung up. "Jean," I said, "cancel all the reservations. I don't have to go after all." I explained what I'd learned.

"This time, it wasn't linked to the product," she said, "but there'll be another time, you know."

I met Judith at the clinic on Friday night. We were going to see a movie and spend the weekend in front of a fire, reading and playing with her new stereo.

"I'm glad you're not going to the East Coast, Michael. It's going to be a nasty weekend—rain and bluster—"

"You okay about me and those guys?" I needed to know.

"I'm still ambivalent, Mike." She took my arm. "But if it really gets bad, you just stop representing them. You're not married to them, after all."

"Interesting analogy, doctor. Very revealing."

"Please, Mike, no Freud. Otherwise, I'll put you in a cage with a sick cat."

Chapter 13

"*F*ifty thousand dollars! What do you mean, you're getting sued for fifty thousand—"

"That's what the letter says, Mike. 'For injuries sustained during the assault on January first, thus requiring corrective surgery.' Jesus."

"Jesus is right," I said. "What the hell did you do? Take a pipe to somebody? David, that's not your style," I said into the phone.

"I guess I should come in and see you, huh?"

"Yeah. Come on in this afternoon and bring the letter. Who's the attorney who sent it?"

"Ken Allen. Know him?"

"Yeah. Pompous horse's ass. But we could have gotten worse. See you later."

David Richards III was a good friend of mine. We played tennis together and went out with his various ladies together. He was heir to old Northwest blue-blood money. His father was president of the family corporation with its contingent of highly respected downtown corporate attorneys.

When I first met David, I had high hopes of wheedling my way into the corporate offices or being David's personal attorney. But in the two years of our friendship, I had written a couple of letters for him about a fender-bender and talked with him about trying to break his trust, which would not disburse funds until he was thirty-two—seven years away. But I hadn't done anything of substance. This afternoon would be interesting

Jean announced him. "Mr. Richards is here to see you, Mr. Tomkins." Then she stepped into my office, pulled the door closed behind her and whispered, "Michael, he doesn't look like he could hurt anybody. He seems like a nice polite person. Should I show him in?"

David slumped in the chair, wearing his usual apparel—jeans, a T-shirt, tennis warm-up jacket. David didn't work. He didn't have to.

"Let me see the letter." He handed it over; I read it. It was short and to the point. "Is this about Susan?"

"Well, yeah. I mean, yeah, I hit her. But she just pissed me off so much I—"

"Let's just wait. We'll talk about the facts in a minute. We have to talk about you and me. Why are you here? If you're here because I'm a friend and you need to talk about this not-small problem, fine. But if you're here as my client and you want me to represent you on this thing, then we have to get certain things straight."

"Such as?"

"Such as why you don't use one of the family attorneys. They won't charge you, and God knows they're competent. Why me?"

"Mike, this thing could get, well, embarrassing." He sat up straighter in his chair, looking more than ever like Robert Redford. "I mean, I did hit Susan. And you've always told me that clients have to be honest with you for you to do the best you can. I don't want to have to be honest with the family lawyers."

"I'll charge you, David. They won't."

He shrugged. "I know."

"You sure you want me to represent you?"

"Tomkins, don't you want to? You sound like you're backing away. Listen, Mike. You know me. You know I'm a dilettante. You know I drink too much, you know I do crazy things and am totally irresponsible. So—"

"For Christ's sake, shut up. You sound like Allen might

sound doing his closing argument to the jury. I'll take the damn case. Now tell me what happened."

Susan and David had been living together off and on for two years. She was a strikingly beautiful girl of twenty-two, with no brains whatsoever. David—bright, articulate, and polished as he was—always gravitated to weird females. Their relationship had deteriorated over its last several months, before the New Year's party they attended about a year ago.

They did not get along at the party. Susan and David both drank too much; they didn't leave the party until two in the morning. While parked in front of the apartment she lived in when she wasn't at David's, they really got into it.

"What does that mean?" I inquired.

"She started saying some really shitty things, and then she went a little berserk."

"Be more specific," I urged.

"I don't know. She started to yell and scream."

I reached for my trusty yellow legal pad. "Go ahead."

"Well, anyway, she really pissed me off, so I hit her a couple of times—in the face."

"With an open hand, I'm sure," I said.

"No. With my fist."

"You can't be sure, though—you were drunk."

"No, Mike, I'm sure. I hit her a couple of times."

"You mean you were defending yourself against her blows, right?"

"Uh . . . I don't know."

"Where did you strike her in self-defense?"

"Oh, Jesus, Mike. It wasn't self-defense. It's just that I got pissed off and gave her a shot."

"This all happened in the front seat of your car?"

"Yes."

"Was Susan wearing shoes?"

"Well, sure—"

"What kind?"

"How the hell do I know? And I don't understand what—"

"High heels, probably," I muttered, writing fast. "You'd just gotten back from a party. Did she try to kick you when she was hitting you?"

"I don't remember—"

"But it's possible, right?"

"Yeah, I guess."

"Okay. When Susan started to hit you did she hurt you?"

"I think so. That's why I—"

"Is it possible that this is what happened? Susan was drunk. Your relationship was breaking up for good. She's always been unstable, and she started to hit and kick you. In order to quiet her down you slapped her twice to try to get her to settle down."

"That doesn't sound like the way—"

"Listen, David. Don't guilt trip yourself into paying a lot of money to Susan. You obviously hit her and caused some damage to her face. She needed plastic surgery. Now, my job is to keep the amount you have to pay to a minimum. If you need to atone for your dastardly deed with coin of the realm, you'll have plenty of opportunity to give it to me."

David smiled. I told him I would call Allen to inform him that I was involved in the case. When I had more information, I'd call David back and pass it along—good or bad.

I picked up the phone right away and got to work. "Ken, Mike Tomkins. I'm calling regarding Susan Adcock."

"Good of you to call, Mike," Allen had the kind of hearty voice I always associate with Rotary Club luncheons. "Pretty serious case."

There was no question in my mind that money would pass in this case. Boy hits girl is never a winner for boy's attorney. But Susan was a banana, and if I had to go the trial (which I didn't think was in David's best interest), I could make her look bad on the witness stand. I knew she wouldn't do well under pressure. But going to trial, with the attendant newspaper coverage—"Scion Belts Playgirl"—would do no one any good. The best way to handle this was to negotiate. "It's not that serious—self-defense. Susan was stoned. David just tried to defend himself when she started hitting him."

"Tomkins, even you wouldn't go to a jury with that preposterous theory. I'm serious, Mike, my client is recovering from a septum rebuild, but the plastic surgeon in L.A. might have to operate a second time. Apparently her airflow is still slightly impaired."

"So, the accidental blow landed on her schnozz."

"Accident! That was an intentional blow. Several, actually. Your client's actions were a textbook case of an intentional tort."

"Well, let's put the question of liability aside. Let's talk realistically about damages. Your demand letter said fifty thousand. Cut the crap with the scare tactics. What are her medical specials?"

"Twenty-six hundred and some change. She's still taking medication, though."

A civil suit involving a tort (civil wrong) involves two phases: liability (who's at fault) and damages (how much is the at-fault party responsible for). If the jury or judge determines that the defendant was not legally liable, then the issue of damages is never reached.

The damage phase of the lawsuit is divided into two parts: special damages (those quantifiable expenses—doctors bills, medications, hospitalization) and general damages (those nonspecific elements that the plaintiff should be compensated for—past and future pain and suffering, scarring, future discomfort, loss of earnings).

"So where in hell did you get fifty thousand? Throw a dart?"

"Mike," Ken said seriously, "Susan had a modeling career, and has suffered a great deal. Obviously, for settlement purposes, I would settle for less to avoid the costs of litigation."

"Okay, Ken, let's talk about the costs of litigation. You said Susan is in L.A.? Her doctor is down there, too?"

"Yes. She moved down there some four months ago."

"You're going to have to spend substantial dollars to bring her doctor up here."

"Hence my offer of a reduced settlement."

"Okay, Allen. Speak to me. Although it's much too early to talk, but—"

"I could recommend around twenty-five thousand."

"Go stuff yourself," I said pleasantly. "Listen, send me the doctor's operative notes. All the medical bills, too. I'll review that stuff with my client."

"Good enough, Mike. But move rapidly. I'm getting pressure to file suit, so—"

"Okay. I'll move rapidly." Jerk.

I spent the next couple of weeks holding David's hand, alternately hearing him say, "Not a nickel to that bitch," or, "Jesus, let's give her what she wants to get rid of this thing."

I spent time in the law library, secure in the knowledge that Jean was in the office answering the phone. I read about similar cases and concluded that the case was worth seven to eighteen thousand dollars. If I got real lucky and could convince a jury that the only reason we were in court was that David had money and Susan wanted it, maybe—just maybe—I could walk out with a defense verdict. Doubtful, but trial attorneys love to dream.

On the other hand, Susan could Valium up and come across as the bruised, beaten lover of a vicious lout. After all, she did have a bent nose. The brain of a small dog, but a bent nose.

"David," I said, "I have a question. Were you living in an apartment at the time of the incident?"

"I don't know. Let me see. Uh, no. I'd gotten rid of my place and that's why I took Susan to her place."

"But you didn't stay with her very much around that time?"

"No. I was staying home, I guess. Yeah, I was staying at home until I could get another place."

"Good."

"Why good?"

"I'll ask the damn questions. Do you have car insurance?"

"Car insurance?"

"What are you, an echo? Yes. Car—automobile—insurance. Did you have it when Susan went down like a rock?"

"I imagine so."

"Okay. Get me your auto policy and ask your parents to send me their homeowners' policy. I know they would have one."

"I don't understand, Mike. What the hell does insurance have to do with this lawsuit?"

"Probably nothing, but I'll try anything to run up your bill. Just send them to me, okay?"

"I'll ask Father to send you his copy."

"Great. And David—cross your fingers."

Auto insurance is a peculiar type of insurance. The coverage section of the policy is much more broad than most people realize. It covers damages evolving from any activity in, on, or around an automobile.

For instance, if you are hit by a car while walking, the pedestrian's own auto insurance will apply if the driver has no insurance. If a tree falls on little Billy while he is in a car, auto insurance is applicable, and will pay his funeral expenses. If grandpa slips on some ice and breaks his dentures while getting into or out of a car, then the car insurance will pay for new ones.

Thus, I thought, since the altercation took place in David's car, maybe this insurance company would pay at least some money. But I had to look at the specific language of the policy to determine how much of a long shot it was.

The leading case in this area involved two deer hunters driving to the forest. The passenger hunter, anxious to kill little brown-eyed creatures, loaded his rifle before reaching the hunting area. The road got rough and the car bumped along. One bump caused the rifle to discharge, killing the driver. The estate sued the auto insurance carrier, alleging that since the accident was auto related, the insurance company was liable to pay. The court, however, said no. The cause of the accident was a discharging rifle. The car had nothing to do with the injury; it was only circumstance that the injury occurred in a car, and thus the auto carrier was not required to pay.

Now, I reasoned that since both Susan and David were drunk, maybe the damage to Susan's nose was done not by David's fist, but by the rearview mirror or door handle in the car.

After receiving David's auto policy and calling the district claims manager, I was informed that the possibility of their coming up with a nickel was slim to nonexistent.

"Didn't you read *Bailey* v. *Sun Auto*?"

"You mean the hunting accident case? Yes I did, and I feel that with these particular facts—"

"Let me stop you right here, Mr. Tomkins. Either you can't read or you're not a member of the bar. Your client's case is worth zero to the company. There is no coverage under the language of the policy or under the facts of your particular case."

"Well, it was worth a try, anyway."

"Perhaps it was, Mr. Tomkins. Call me when you have a better case."

He was right.

I still had not received David's father's homeowners' policy.

"How come, David? I asked over two weeks ago."

"Father thinks it's a stupid waste of his time, your time, and my money."

"Is he home? Put him on the line."

I waited. David's father was in his early sixties, a portly gentleman who always spoke to the point in a rather brusque manner. He generally didn't interfere in David's life, perhaps because he didn't understand it and didn't have the time to learn. We had exchanged approximately one hundred words since I met David, such as "Please shut the door, son." "Yes, sir."

He picked up the phone. "Yes?"

"Mr. Richards? I'm Mike Tomkins, David's attorney."

"I know that. We've met?"

I sure know how to impress people. "Yes, on several occasions."

"Well, what is it?"

"I asked David to get copies of your homeowners' policies so I could—"

"Excuse me, but I don't see how my policy has any bearing on David's troubles."

"Well, I'm not sure it does either, sir. But I have an angle that might help get David out of this jam—"

"It would seem to me that David's money is better spent—"

I'd had about enough of this pompous ass. I didn't give a shit what the old goat thought of me, but I had better things to do than justify myself to him. "Mr. Richards, I don't have any idea why you are so resistant to giving me your policy, and I do not appreciate getting cross-examined about my strategy. I have been retained by your son to do the best I can, check out every possibility. If you don't want to help those people who are trying to help your son, I suggest you get counsel that you approve of. I don't need to fight you, too."

"If you insist, Mr. Tomkins, I will send you my policy—for all the good it will do. I wouldn't be honest, however, if I did not say that an older and more experienced attorney might well approach this case quite differently. It will serve no purpose to have this affair dragged about in the courts. We are quite well known, as you are aware."

I slammed down the phone and sat drumming my fingertips on my desk.

"I couldn't help overhearing," said Jean, coming in and sinking down into the client chair. "He was pretty rough on you, wasn't he?"

It was a comfortable thing to have Jean around. There was always somebody to talk to, for one thing—somebody who knew what was going on most of the time and could listen with a critical ear. I told her about my theory. Homeowners' insurance *was* a long shot, but one I felt was worth exploring. Homeowners' policies ordinarily cover any person of the insured's family who is living at home. Thus, if David was living at home on the date of the incident, perhaps insurance money could help with (if not totally pay for) Susan's injury. That kind of coverage pays for more than such things as stolen televisions; it also covers grandma falling off the roof or little Tommy accidentally poking out the eye of the kid next door.

Jean wrinkled her forehead. "Isn't the operative word *accidentally*? I'm under the impression that insurance companies will not cover an intentional act."

"Yeah. That's the problem. But I've looked through my notes and I'm sure that although David *thinks* he hit Susan on purpose, for my purposes his fist may have struck her accidentally."

"I can see your reasoning, Michael. It was very clever of you to think of it. I've never heard of anybody using a homeowners' policy that way before. Would you like me to get Mr. Allen on the line?"

Jean was such a comfort. "Sure," I said, grinning. "It's time we had a meeting."

Having Jean around had certainly simplified my life, just as she'd told me it would when I first met her. She knew her business, and I was grateful. There are too few like her left. I had the feeling that she had once had to carve her own niche out in the world and that she would always be able to understand why making moral judgments was a luxury I couldn't afford. I suspected that Jean would consider it immoral to make those judgments at all.

I had spoken to very few nonattorneys about my growing feelings about the practice of law. And when I had, no one had listened. Too many television dramas, maybe—so they thought they already knew. The quick reaction to my theory about the difference being small between what I had to offer the world and what a mom and pop grocery store offered it came down to the implication that I was a crass opportunist who had become a lawyer for the money.

Professions in the seventies and eighties have changed dramatically, probably as a result of the whole system of education. It seems that everyone is a professional with some years of college and some sort of a ticket—bar card, M.D., A.A., M.B.A.

The really valuable people in the world now are those who produce something and have a skill. Jean made a real difference to my practice. She was a real professional.

Who the hell types anymore? Men still think it's not a manly thing to do; women are counseled by their liberated sisters not to admit they know how. The ranks of secretaries are dwindling. The old pros like Jean are gradually being replaced by the young high school graduates who can't type, can't spell, can't use a dictionary to check their errors. Since being a secretary is considered such a degrading job now, there are very few of them left who will even admit they take it seriously.

My generation was pushed into college to hedge against the next depression: "If you have that piece of paper, you can always get a job." As it turns out, that wasn't necessarily the truth. For a lot of us, the degree is of no practical value.

Secretarial salaries will continue to rise to meet the demand for that kind of very personalized, ultraspecialized skill. I was glad Jean had found me.

I met Allen in a bar near his office after work. He came in

all tweedy, his Gucci shoes clacking on the parquet floors. He placed his leather attaché case on the empty chair between us and ordered a Gibson "dry, very dry."

I ordered a Coke float. "Wet, very wet."

The waitress looked bored. "We don't have those here."

"Okay. Bring me a beer. Since I'm paying for the pleasure of this man's company, a little beer will do."

Ken didn't smile. He was so up tight. I felt that he needed to smile more, and I hoped that he would do just that as I laid my proposal before him. I waited for our drinks to come and took a sip of my beer. "Ken, I've done some research since I spoke to you last. I've gone over David's economic position with him in some detail, spoken to his trust officers, and—"

"Get to the point, Mike," Ken interrupted, looking at his gold watch.

"David doesn't have any money to settle, no assets at all, really."

"What the hell are you trying to pull, Tomkins?"

"Just listen. I've got bad news and good news. All of David's money is in trust. He hasn't worked in six months, and when he does he doesn't last long. No self-discipline, I think—"

"That's for sure," said Ken morosely, signaling for another round.

"Just shut up, Allen, okay? Let me finish."

He finished his drink with a gulp. "Okay."

"If you file suit and go to trial you may well win—but not be able to collect. On the other hand, I could get lucky and walk out with a defense verdict."

"Not likely, Tomkins, not likely at all." He stirred the onion around in his fresh drink, a smug look on his face.

"So, for the sake of argument," I continued, "you win thirty-five thousand—or even twenty thousand. We file for bankruptcy, and you still can't get at the trust moneys."

"I knew you hadn't passed the bar, Tomkins. One cannot discharge an obligation in federal bankruptcy court if that obligation—as it would be in this case—is a judgment for an intentional tort. Only judgments for negligent tortious actions can be discharged. I would still have six years to execute on the judgment. Not, mind you, that I believe for a second that David's penniless."

"So what do you do, Allen? You then get your client involved in another lawsuit trying to prevent discharge in bankruptcy court and/or trying to break David's trust, and still no sign of money for little Susan's face." I finished my first beer, started on my second. "And by the way, if your client has enough smarts to be a model, you have enough personality to be a talk-show host."

"You asked me for this drink so you could offer to settle for nothing? And then insult me?"

"Not so fast. I have an idea. If it works, everybody wins. And I mean everybody."

"That can't possibly be. Lawsuits are brought for losers and winners. Everyone can't win."

"Thank you, professor. Now just listen." I took a sip of my beer. "David was living at home on January first. His parents have a homeowners' policy. David is covered." I let that lie there, waiting for it to sink in. "Now, if Susan's injury was a result of an accidental blow, or maybe Susan turned to the rearview mirror while both our clients were engaged in an admittedly heated argument . . ." I let the sentence trail off. Ken Allen was no dummy.

"Continue, Mike." He sounded interested.

"Thank you. The question comes down to Susan. What does she want? That's always been the real question. If she wants money, I think you and I cooperating can get her paid off quickly. Not in fifteen months when this thing gets to court. If she wants to drag David through the mud—get back at him, the woman scorned thing—then it will cost her a bundle. She may even lose, and you don't get paid for a long time, if at all. The attendant publicity could hurt everyone, no money goes to anyone except the expert witnesses." I took a deep breath. "In other words, if she says it was not intentional, the insurance company would probably kick in to help her."

"Hmmm." Allen chewed on a plastic toothpick. "What's wrong with this scheme? Where are the gambles?"

"There are several. For one thing, the insurance company can disbelieve our theory of the case and refuse coverage. But from your point of view, here's the only gamble: You admit that the injury was accidental and then if the insurance company doesn't come through, you gamble David won't go bankrupt if he loses in court. Susan's judgment against David would be dischargeable at that point."

"So it comes down to Susan."

"It always has. How well can you control your client and maneuver her to make the right decision?"

"What do you mean, 'right'? Right for you, you mean."

"Listen, Ken. If your client doesn't want a quick and fair payout, then you have no business prosecuting this as a grudge match. Plus, if I were you, I wouldn't want to tie my one-third contingency fee to a crazy lady who wants a pound of flesh much more than she wants cash. Just explain to Susan the risks of going to trial."

"Don't tell me how to deal with my client," Ken said testily.

"Okay. Don't get excited. I'll even buy you another drink. Just mull over what I've said."

Later, watching Allen sip through half his drink, I tried to guess whether his pride would allow him to admit the idea had merit.

Finally he spoke. "So where do you go from here, assuming I agree to all this?"

"I call Northwest Insurance Company and start the ball rolling. You call Susan and start twisting some arms. But let's talk realistically about dollars. Northwest is not going to come up with anything like twenty-five thousand. I'll try to get as much as possible, but more than likely twelve to seventeen is the range. Okay?"

"Why do I feel like I'm getting bent over, Tomkins?"

"Because you don't like trusting me. But you've got to. You think I like working my ass off to make you money?"

"Okay, Tomkins. You're uncomfortable. I'm uncomfortable. So call me when I can pick up my check." He fondled his leather briefcase, tucked it under his arm, and left.

The next morning I called Northwest Insurance Company and asked to speak to a supervisor in the claims department. This case had enough wrinkles in it already, and I knew a supervisor was going to get involved sooner or later. It took several days before the supervisor got back to me. During that time I called Allen to continuously reassure him. David called from time to time to ask "How much will I have to pay?"

When the supervisor did call, he wanted a statement from the claimant Susan as to exactly what happened. "You know, Mr. Tomkins, we're not sure this thing was accidental at all. And if it wasn't—well, as you know there's no coverage."

I called Allen. "Well, it's getting down to the short hairs."

"Meaning?"

"Meaning we have to give Northwest Insurance a written statement of the event. Based on that statement, I think they'd come across fairly soon. So . . . have you talked to Susan?"

"Yes, I have."

"So?"

"So, she's ambivalent."

"Also a fool who's blowing twelve to fifteen thousand dollars." I was furious. "Well, okay, then. I'm not going to waste any more of my goddamn time with this thing trying to put money in both of your pockets. File your lawsuit, Allen. I'm going to want to take Susan's deposition in my office within fifteen days. So inform your client that she's going to be spending some time in the great Northwest at her own expense. I'll advise my client not to offer you a penny out of his pocket prior to trial. Since we can't settle this thing early and inexpensively, we might as well go all the way."

I was really angry. I had built a perfect house of cards, and now because Allen couldn't control his greedy client, my cardhouse was collapsing. I felt like drafting the goddamn letter myself and sending it to the insurance company.

"Don't get angry at me, Mike. To tell you the truth I'm a bit disappointed myself. I actually did feel that the result we proposed was a fair and equitable one. But Susan feels that David deserves—uh, let me rephrase that."

"No need, Allen. You've told me enough. But let me say this: I know Susan well enough to believe that she has done some pretty bizarre things in the past and that if there are any proverbial skeletons in her closet, and my tummy tells me that's a pretty big closet, I'm going to find those skeletons and rattle some bones."

"You know nothing, Tomkins. And I will not pass on your veiled threats to Susan, who has the perfect right to see justice done in the manner that she feels—"

"Cut the crap, Allen. Jesus, sometimes you drive me crazy. All I'm saying is this: I'm going to trial on this one and I'm going to drag sweet blue-eyed Susan through the mud. And in this double-standard society of ours, David will walk away relatively unscarred. Susan will be bloody as hell. I'm not so sure twelve middle-class jurors are going to be very sympathetic to Susan and want to give her barrels of money."

"You would have said something to me before this if you had anything." Allen sounded nervous.

"Why? I was trying to cooperate. Before this, anyway. Listen, I've got to go and do something profitable—like walk my dog. I'll send over the subpoenas for the deposition."

Four days later I received a letter from Allen. It read: "Enclosed please find a copy of the letter required by Northwest Insurance Company."

And damned if the thing didn't recite chapter and verse,

using the very language I would have used if I'd written the damn thing myself.

I had gotten lucky. Apparently I had thrown so much stuff against the wall that something had stuck. Susan knew of skeletons I had only guessed at.

After several more days of discussion with the insurance company, we both agreed that *they* should offer Susan thirteen thousand, five hundred. They wanted David to come up with some money as contribution. I quickly disabused them of that notion. "Remember," I said, "David's paying my fee. He already *is* contributing to the pot."

I called my good friend Ken Allen and told him they wanted to settle, but only if it could be done expeditiously, as their costs were mounting. He bought thirteen five as a good settlement involving little or no out-of-pocket costs to his firm. It was settled.

"Is David there, please?"

"Who's calling, please?"

"Mike Tomkins. Uh, Mr. Richards?"

"Yes."

"Is David there? Something has come up—"

"I hope it's not too negative."

You old bastard. "Well, Sir, it's hard to say, actually."

"I'll tell him you called. He's at the tennis club. By the way, I spoke to Mr. Paul Phillips of Phillips and Hart about our homeowners' theory. Quite candidly, he felt—"

"Uh, excuse me, Mr. Richards. I have a call on the other line. Tell David to call me back? Thanks."

I smiled a little—then a lot.

Chapter 14

Judith and I were having a late breakfast, reading the Sunday paper. Prosser was in the living room, watching the game on TV. He was always a great sports fan, but he wasn't much fun to watch with. He didn't understand the rules very well. Judith never did understand why I always bothered to explain.

I turned to the real estate section. It had stopped raining, and promised to be a relatively dry (for Seattle) and windy day. The past few months I had started looking at houses with an idea of buying one. I always felt that a house is for an adult to live in—an adult with a spouse and some children. But times were changing. Unmarried types were buying houses too. It was too good an investment to put off much longer, and since I was still busy at the office and gathering a certain measure of economic security, I was beginning to take a hard look at the weekly listings.

"Do you have to go into the clinic today?" I asked.

"No, but I want to go to my place and check the mail," she said, frowning at an editorial. "Why?"

"I thought we could go to the aquarium or something like that, maybe look at a house. Sunday things to do."

"House?" She put down the paper.

"Yeah. Prosser wants a yard of his own. So do I. How about you?"

"Meaning?"

"What I said. You want to live in a house sometime?"

"Well, sure, Mike. Sometime. But where I don't know. I'm not sure where I'll be in a year or two. Why set roots if you're not sure?"

"Thinking about your Yerkes application?"

"Uh-huh. Sometimes I want to go very badly. Sometimes I hope they tell me to take a hike. Then sometimes, like now, I'm ambivalent as hell."

There was nothing I could say. I gave her a kiss. After we cleared the dishes away, we drove to her apartment. The mailbox was full.

"Well, here it is," she said.

I recognized the Yerkes envelope. My stomach lurched. I felt like it was the letter from the bar association. "Thick or thin?" I asked.

"Who the hell cares. Dumb stupid question. Jesus!" She sat down abruptly on the couch. Her upper lip was covered with tiny beads of perspiration.

"Easy there, girl—"

"I'm not a horse, dammit." She stared at the envelope. "Oh, Mike, I'm sorry. What difference does it make how thick it is?"

"Thick is always better than thin. Tomkins' Rule."

She hefted the envelope. "Terrific. Thin as a whisker."

"Is that vet talk? Open the damn thing, Judith."

She did, pulling out one sheet of rich parchment which crackled in her hand as her eyes raced over the three short paragraphs typed there. I looked over her shoulder.

If she wanted to be a Georgia peach and hang around gorillas she could, and they'd even pay her to do so.

"Shit," she said.

"I'm sorry. Tomkins' Rule is just that—a rule. It's not a law." I kissed her. "Congratulations. Those apes won't know what hit them. You'll have them reading at a sixth-grade level in no time."

She hugged me. "I really have to decide now, don't I? The other way, all decisions were made for me. This adult business is the pits." She was quiet for a minute. "If I say yes, I'll leave in three weeks."

"They don't mess around, do they?" I stood. "Well, I guess you have some decisions to make in the days ahead. But it is a nice situation to be in—you can't really lose. Listen. You stay here and think. If I stay, I'll probably beg you to stay, crawling on my knees—"

"Thanks, Mike. I do need some time. Maybe I'll get into my favorite robe, crawl into a fetal position and write some prescriptions." She pulled me down and kissed me, but I could tell she was already thinking it over.

I didn't call her for several days. I told myself it was because I didn't want to poison the well. Of course that was crap. I wanted to poison the bloody hell out of that well. Knowing I had no self control, I worked like a madman, staying late, catching up on the trivial tasks that always get shoved to the bottom of the stack. Working hard and snarling at Lamb and Jean took up most of my time.

"Line two, Mr. Grumpy." Jean stood in my office door. "She wants to know if you're busy."

"Well, Jean—here it is." I hesitated before pushing the blinking button. "What do you think? Me, or a hairy guy who craves bananas?"

"Whatever she does, Michael, will be the best thing for her." Jean turned to go back to her desk. "Good luck."

The going-away party for Judith was intimate, fun, and very boozy. Her apartment was entirely denuded of all signs of her past life. New tenant time. I hadn't been sure how to break the news to Prosser that he was going to lose his surrogate mother, so I'd said nothing to him. But he knew. He didn't let Judith out of his sight the whole evening, following her around with a mournful look in his brown eyes.

Her plane was to leave at six the following morning. After the party, we loaded her two traveling bags into my car and drove to my place for the last time. For a while, anyway.

"I'm going to miss you, babe. You know that. Losing my lady to a bunch of apes isn't the easiest thing in the world to take in stride." The streets were almost deserted this time of night. Traffic lights made smears of gaudy color reflected in the rain on the pavement.

"Don't, okay?" Janet stared out the side window. "I don't want to go. When I get there, it'll be okay, but I hate meeting new people, new situations. I'm not very good at that sort of thing."

"Oh? I never noticed. I remember the first time we met. You were warm, open—"

She laughed. "Bastard." When she leaned over to kiss my cheek, Prosser thrust his ninety-pound head between us, the better to peer through the windshield. "I'm going to miss both of you so much," Judith said, hugging him.

"Jean," I called, "take a letter." I was at my desk working on a subrogation file. "Re Cascade Casualty versus Pronesti—"

"Oh, yes," said Jean, snapping her steno pad closed in disgust. "That's a biggie. If we're lucky, we'll make thirty bucks on it. Go home, Michael. There's nothing that important that you can't leave. John can do the dissolution this afternoon. You're not doing anybody any good here anyway."

"Yeah, maybe I will," I said. "I can't seem to concentrate anyway."

"You're a pathetic creature today—lovesick at twenty-five. She'll be back, you know. She'll be back." Jean handed me my raincoat. "Go on now. Take Prosser for a walk."

I was on my way out when the phone buzzed. I paused, ignoring Jean's motions toward the front door. "If it's an ape calling from the South," I told her, "take a cage number. I'll call him back."

"No," Jean said into the phone, "there's no Tom Kins here. It's Michael Tomkins. No, no, he's a lawyer, not an insurance adjustor. One moment, please, I'll see." She pushed the hold button. "Do you know a Mrs. Carlyle?"

"Edna? Edna Carlyle, for the love of God?"

"Yes. A client?"

"Yeah," I said, laughing. "An old one. A real old one. Get it?"

"No." Jean reached for the phone. "I'll tell her you aren't in today."

"Wait," I said, tossing my coat toward the coatrack. "I'll take it." What the hell, I thought, as I went back to take the call. Maybe I'll have her drive down to the new office. I can always use the business.